MAKE YOUR OWN MAGIC

MAKE YOUR OWN MAGIC

MAGIC

DISCOVER THE SECRET TRICKS OF A TIKTOK MAGICIAN

JOEL M

HarperCollinsPublishers

CONTENTS

HarperCollins*Publishers*
1 London Bridge Street, London SE1 9GF

www.harpercollins.co.uk

HarperCollins*Publishers*
1st Floor, Watermarque Building, Ringsend Road,
Dublin 4, Ireland

First published by HarperCollins*Publishers* 2021

1 3 5 7 9 10 8 6 4 2

© Joel Mawhinney 2021
Illustrations © Sarah Leuzzi
Design and layout by Louise Leffler
Photographs © Beau Cremer
Personal photographs courtesy of the author.

Joel Mawhinney asserts the moral right to be identified
as the author of this work

MIX
Paper from
responsible sources
FSC™ C007454

FSC
www.fsc.org

This book is produced from independently certified FSC™ paper
to ensure responsible forest management.

For more information visit: www.harpercollins.co.uk/green

This book is produced from independently certified FSCTM
paper to ensure responsible forest management.

For more information visit:
www.harpercollins.co.uk/green

WELCOME

A question for you: what five-letter word can you remove two letters from and yet it still has the same meaning?

Lovely to meet you, wonderful reader! I hope that little riddle got your attention. If you stick around, I'll even give you the answer ...

Oh, what a tease. You see, this has been my obsession since I was a child. I love presenting people with a puzzle, and not divulging the secret – to their annoyance and to my own great personal satisfaction.

Not so here in this book, however. In fact, for the first time, I'll be taking you behind the curtain, telling you what it's like growing up as the odd one out and, hopefully, teaching you a few tricks along the way.

Exceedingly unlikely as it may be – if you happened to open this book without glancing at the front cover, allow me to briefly introduce myself.

My name is Joel Mawhinney, though I go by Joel M. (Apparently, Mawhinney doesn't fit nicely on promotional posters.) I'm a twenty-three-year-old from Northern Ireland, who enjoys reading, playing the piano, eating as many burrito bowls as my metabolism allows and, most importantly, loves the world of magic.

And now, so it seems, I'm an author, too. How bizarre! I hope my old English teacher is proud of me.

Between the first and last pages of this little volume are stories, confessions and secrets from my twenty-three years of life to date. The world of a magician is an unusual one, to say the least and, if nothing else, I hope you'll find my adventures entertaining, so that the embarrassment I've gone through in reliving some of the more cringeworthy memories was worth it.

So what does the life of a young magician look like? Well, stick around and I'll show you. You're going to learn the secrets behind some of my favourite magic tricks and how to perform them for an audience, confounding and astounding them. Along the way, you'll also glean some magical tips on how to turn yourself into an internet sensation, creating content that goes viral and transforming your life for the better. Because although I've only been on this planet for a relatively short time, I've had the (sometimes questionable) pleasure of some very unusual yet valuable experiences – things that I have learned from so that you, luckily, won't have to.

Now, as for that riddle – the answer is in plain sight. But did you catch it? If you did, you're wired to be a magician. If not, you might want to pay even closer attention in future.

Sorry, I couldn't resist a little enigma.*

Joel M
Belfast, 19 June 2021

*Pay attention to the italics.

THE CASE

OF THE

VANISHING

ENGAGEMENT

RING

The question I get asked the most (besides 'Tell me this week's winning lottery numbers,' or, 'Can you make my husband disappear?') is: 'How did you do that?'

As a modern-day wizard, that much is to be expected. But a question I am asked almost as often, and usually with more genuine curiosity, is: 'Have you ever got a trick wrong?'

And the answer to that is yes. Absolutely, unequivocally yes. More times than I'd care to admit! But as a mentor of mine often says: 'If you aren't messing tricks up, you're definitely not doing enough gigs.'

Mistakes are bound to happen when you're toying with the impossible, especially when you're dealing with other human beings. Over the years, I've tried to reduce the number of blunders that will inevitably occur, but I have yet to become immune to them.

I've had plenty of horror stories, but allow me to take you back to one in particular, when I was but an honest, fresh-faced eight-year-old.

At this point, I had been practising magic for a few years. Given that it was about the only thing I had discovered myself to be good at, I worked hard at it, and had already become a fairly competent sleight-of-hand magician.

Let me stress, I was – no, sorry, I still am – *useless* at everything else. And I mean useless. But at any rate, by the ripe age of eight, I had a cute magic show prepared and polished, ready for the world to see. And by *the world*, of course I mean immediate family and maybe some friends. Let's not get ahead of ourselves here.

My little show spanned twenty minutes and included tricks such as the classic 'Cups and Balls', the 'Vanishing Knot' and 'Playing Card into Balloon'. (The latter practically built up my self-esteem.)

So there I was: eight years old, and ready to jump right into the glamorous world of showbiz. Or so I thought. And the opportunity came in the form of my uncle's wedding.

Looking back, it is super funny that my uncle decided to choose me as the primary (and also free) form of entertainment for his big day. No hate; I love an opportunist.

Being asked to do work for free, or for 'exposure', is common when you're trying to make it in the world of entertainment. And it's the best place to start in this field, particularly at the age of eight. So I gratefully accepted the job. To say I was excited would be a tremendous understatement.

The wedding was to take place in Cyprus, so naturally my family made a holiday out of it. What a treat.

Me, Emma (sister) and Ethan (brother) in Cyprus, ready for the wedding.

I stuffed my Marvin's Magic bag full of ropes, scissors, balloons, cards, tape, magnets and all sorts of mystical gizmos. As you can imagine, I caused a major stir going through airport security – something that has never become easier over the years. I've yet to make it through without causing some sort of commotion.

One short flight later, and we'd arrived in sunny Cyprus. Two weeks of sun, fun and, eventually . . . embarrassment. You'll see.

Skipping over the usual holiday antics, I finally found myself at the wedding. My job for the day was to act as the entertainment in two particular ways. Firstly, I would be performing my prepared magic show for all the guests, just after the speeches, at the front of the room. Secondly, I would be roaming the after party, performing close-up magic for each individual table. The usual wedding magician set-up.

My very gracious uncle gave me a lovely little intro, and I was off. My time had come. I was ready to jump from total obscurity into wedding stardom. Obviously, no matter how good – or bad – my little show was, all the adults were going to applaud and encourage me. I was oblivious to this, however. For me it was time to amaze.

I kicked off the show with a bang, and everything went incredibly well. No major mishaps and all the tricks worked. Bravo. I do have a vague recollection of my show having gone on for about five minutes too long . . . some passing comment from my dear mother about 'leave them wanting more'. But all in all, a total success. Lots of applause, lots of laughter.

I was on cloud nine. Part one of my first official magic show under my belt! Not too shabby for an eight-year-old. What could possibly go wrong to knock me off this fluffy little cloud of joy?

Again, you'll see.

I took a short break before getting into my role as roaming close-up magician. One glass of orange cordial and I was set to go, still high on the adrenaline of my previous accomplishment.

Now, if you've never had the pleasure of stumbling across a close-up magician, let me break down what it is that we do. Or, at the very least, what we're *supposed* to do.

Let's say, you're sitting with some friends. You're all having a lovely time, catching up, telling stories and spreading the latest and greatest gossip. Well, it's my job to entirely disrupt that, by suggesting that you would *just love* to watch a card trick.

You know . . . people always tell me that it seems like such an amazing job, being a magician. And in many ways it is. I love it. But I would challenge you to find any rational person who would willingly spend the majority of their time interrupting groups of strangers, then proving their worth to said strangers, over and over and over again. That said, I still seem to enjoy it. But I've yet to find more than twenty other people who do. It truly is a nerve-wracking job.

Let's get back to the story.

I was on fire. (I probably wasn't, but my ego has firmly locked that image into my mind over the years, so I'm sticking to it.) I was dazzling the crowd, group after group, showing off my finest close-up illusions. From card tricks to coin tricks, from mind reading to metal bending – I was in my element. I hadn't messed up a single trick. Yet.

And there it was. The corner table.

I remember it vividly. That one table, looming larger than all the rest, with more people seated at it than three other tables rolled into one. This was the group to impress. This was my prize. Shoulders back, deep breath in and into battle.

'Hello everyone,' said the cute eight-year-old me. 'I'm your magician for the evening, can I show you a trick?' Among all the *awws* and *ahhhs* came a definite 'yes'. So I jumped into my close-up routine.

At that time, my absolute favourite close-up magic stunt was the 'teleporting ring trick'. I always saved it for special occasions because it's such a pain to pull off. Lots of prep, but a massive pay-off. Let me break it down for you.

The magician borrows a finger ring. The magician vanishes the ring. The ring reappears on the stem of a wine glass. An impossible feat. Memorable and jaw-dropping.

I didn't create the trick, so I feel totally comfortable bragging about it. It's awesome. And it was the only trick I needed to floor the group at the big table.

'May I borrow your ring, madam?' I asked one of the women at the table.

With the consent of the very kind woman who was seated right at the centre of the group (a little tactic for you young magicians), I took the ring and placed it in my fist.

Two things.

Firstly, this particular ring was very, very expensive. I didn't know that at the time, of course, but my mother was soon to enlighten me. Secondly, please remember that I was only eight years old, with very little experience and even less common sense.

I squeezed the ring inside my fist, blew on the back of my hand, and . . . ta-da, the ring was gone. Thunderous applause met my ears!

Such was my excitement, that I decided to perform another magic trick to increase the time between the vanishing of the ring and its reappearance. Best to make the most of such a magical moment.

Out came my trusty deck of cards, and very soon I was five minutes deep into my favourite routine, using the fifty-two pyrotechnic pasteboards that had obsessively consumed my youth.

Even more thunderous applause. Things couldn't have gone better! I took my bow (which I strangely used to do when I was a child, even when in small groups) and confidently strode towards the next eager group.

Just a moment. Did you notice anything? I certainly didn't at the time.

I was three-quarters of the way through the final table for the night when I felt a gentle tap on my shoulder.

'I'm so sorry to interrupt you, Joel, but my fiancée was wondering where you might have put her engagement ring? We assumed that you were going to make it reappear and we didn't want spoil the fun too early.'

Ah.

You see, the trouble was, I *had* made the ring vanish. Not only from my closed fist, but from my own memory. To this very day, I have absolutely no recollection of ever borrowing that engagement ring. I must have been so high on self-admiration that the moment passed me by.

'What ring?' I asked.

'Good one, kid,' said the gentleman, 'but we really do need that ring back. It's very important to us.'

'I'm so sorry, but I really have no idea what you're talking about,' I replied. And it was true. I was clueless as to what the gentleman was talking about. In my mind, I had never borrowed a ring.

At this point the poor man had to choose between shouting at the nephew of the groom or politely returning, empty-handed, to his fiancée. He chose the latter. What a legend.

I finished up at the final table and began to pack up my magic bag. That was when I felt the second tap on my shoulder. It was my mother. Bless my mother, she is the most patient, loving, kind woman you'll ever meet. But in this case, she looked worried.

'Joel, son, can you please give back that ring you took? It's not funny any more. That poor lady is really worried.'

'I didn't take a ring from her!' I exclaimed, in my squeaky eight-year-old voice. Now things were starting to heat up.

I knew that I hadn't borrowed the ring. Sadly for me, however, about fifteen people had seen me take it. And, believe it or not, the word of fifteen adults tends to hold some weight against that of an eight-year-old wannabe magician.

My disbelieving mother searched my bag and came up dry. Nothing. I was asked to retrace my steps, but there was no sign of the hidden gem.

Over the speakers, my mortified uncle announced to the room that there was a missing engagement ring, and that he'd massively appreciate it if everyone would stop what they were doing and get busy finding it. Bless his soul – he didn't tell the guests that it was, in fact, me who had lost it.

And so the search began.

Under the tables, inside the toilets, even the hotel swimming pool was searched, but no luck. About an hour went by, and no one had found the ring. Of course, I was so convinced that I was blameless in the whole affair that I barely bothered to glance around.

I'm going to practise more magic, I thought to myself. Must get my deck of cards out.

And, as I reached into my pocket and pulled out my deck of cards . . .

Ding

From underneath the cards fell the very engagement ring that everyone was looking for. I was in shock.

Up until that point I would have sworn on my life that I'd never touched that ring. I was convinced I could have passed a lie-detector test. But quite clearly, I had placed it in my pocket in a quick moment of misdirection and forgotten.

So. What to do now?

Like any good eight-year-old, I ran, teary-eyed, to my mother. I can still remember the look of relief on her face when I pulled out that ring. I could tell she believed me when I said I didn't remember taking it. After all, I was such a clueless child, always in my own little world.

So the ring was quietly returned, and my uncle announced that it had been found. And the best part of the story is that the kind lady whose ring I had borrowed pretended to have found it herself, underneath her seat, so that I – the thief – could save face. Another legend.

To this very day, I have never borrowed another engagement ring for a magic trick. That trauma isn't going anywhere any time soon. And the moral? Don't touch what you can't afford, kids.

So once again, to answer the question, 'Do you ever get a trick wrong?' Yes. Not as often these days, but yes. And have no fear – this is only the first of many horror stories to come. Buckle your seatbelts.

YOU SEE, THE TROUBLE WAS, I HAD MADE THE RING VANISH. NOT ONLY FROM MY CLOSED FIST, BUT FROM MY OWN MEMORY. TO THIS VERY DAY, I HAVE ABSOLUTELY NO RECOLLECTION OF EVER BORROWING THAT ENGAGEMENT RING. I MUST HAVE BEEN SO HIGH ON SELF-ADMIRATION THAT THE MOMENT PASSED ME BY.

RING VANISH
(VANISHING ENGAGEMENT RING)

I recommend extreme caution when borrowing another person's belongings, but making an ordinary object disappear is worth the risk! And while I may have made an engagement ring disappear for slightly too long, that shouldn't stop you from trying.

You're going to need to practise this one quite a lot before it looks good. But once you get it down, you'll never ever be stuck for an incredible piece of magic that you can do any time, anywhere.

More than just making a ring vanish, this is a little routine, packaged up and ready to perform. So grab a ring, and let's get started.

THE TRICK

Here's what happens:

- You borrow a ring from someone in your audience and pop it on your thumb.

- In full view, place the ring underneath your arm, trapping it between your arm and body.

- You ask the audience if they think it would be possible for you to somehow flick the ring up into the air and catch it on your finger. The ultimate trick shot. Not impossible, but unlikely! The people in the audience naturally say 'No' (unless they have unusual faith in your abilities).

- You concentrate, and then relax the arm that is hiding the ring away from the side of your body. Expecting the ring to clatter to the floor, the spectators will often make a rush to catch the trinket. But the ring has vanished into thin air, despite having clearly been placed under your arm.

- You show that the ring has appeared on your opposite hand! The spectators go wild, you crowd-surf across the nation and the Queen of England herself makes a special visit to congratulate you on your incredible performance.

Reaction not guaranteed

THE SECRET

Before we get into the routine, and how to present it, you need to learn one move. It shouldn't take much time to master, but I recommend practising it in front of a mirror or in front of a camera to see things from the perspective of the audience.

- Position your hand in the 'thumbs-up' position, then place the ring on your thumb and show it clearly (see photo 3 overleaf).

Now comes the sneaky bit . . .

- In the motion of *placing the ring under your arm*, you secretly steal it away into your other fist. To do this, simply lower your thumb, and use your other fingers to grab it away (see photos 5 and 6). The way you operate the move will largely depend on your hand size, but practise until you can do it without thinking. The key here is to operate the secret move while you have the distraction of your arm. The bigger action of moving your entire arm covers the smaller motion of you concealing the ring. The visual contrast of the ring being momentarily on your finger and then gone creates a very convincing illusion.

Of course, a huge part of selling the illusion lies in acting as though the ring is securely underneath your arm. You can do this by clenching your arm close to your body, as though any movement would cause the ring to fall. Although you can make this trick work in almost all situations, it is easier to perform in some sort of clothing that covers your arm. All attention should be drawn to your arm, squeezed to your body.

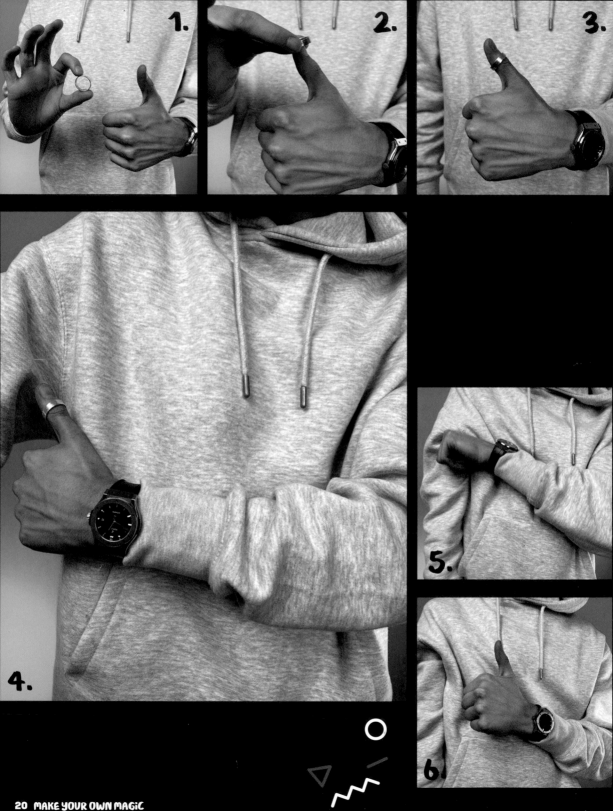

7.

8.

- Now, while attention is off your hand secretly concealing the ring, you'll have the chance to manoeuvre it on to one of your fingers (see photo 7). It doesn't matter which, although I'd recommend that you don't place it back on the thumb. It may lead some people to question whether it ever really left in the first place!

- All that's left to do now, is to act. The more effort you put into building up the reveal, the better. With this in mind, I choose to present this as a challenge trick where I bet the audience that I can flick the ring from underneath my arm into the air and catch it on my finger. That way, they're conditioned to expect a certain outcome, and the ring vanishing will truly take them by surprise.

When revealing that the ring has returned to my hand, I choose to be bold and rest my hand in a place that should have made it so obvious that the ring was there. But stay within your comfort zone. I'm personally happy to leave my hand on the table, right in front of the audience, knowing they won't be looking for it, with all their attention on my other arm. It's all down to confidence.

Well, that's it. I hope you have fun learning, rehearsing and practising this little trick. It's a lot of fun, and dead simple to do.

Just don't *lose* the ring.

Or do – and sell it on eBay!

I BROKE
HIS
KNUCKLES!

For the most part, I enjoyed school. I don't remember all that much about the early years, but I do recall performing magic in front of my school assembly when I was in Primary Year 6. With all year groups watching, I stood at the front, with my squeaky voice and Mohican hair. (The Mohican was something I embarrassingly insisted on in my younger years, to the horror of my poor mother and headteacher, and to the detriment of my school photographs. It looked like I'd had my hair clamped in a door.)

Pulling out a deck of cards, I invited the deputy head to join me on stage. He towered over me, but never having been too intimidated by adults, I confidently asked him to pick a card. He did so, and showed it to everyone in the assembly hall. Then I asked him to place it back inside the deck and to shuffle.

Something I really miss about being young is that absolutely no one has any faith in your abilities. (Or maybe that was just my experience; in fairness, the hair probably didn't instill much confidence!) People not believing in my magical prowess always led to more fun on my part. With lower expectations, I could over-deliver. Always worked a charm.

I took a guess at the deputy head's card.

I was wrong.

On purpose. But nobody else knew that.

My schoolmates began to laugh and point fingers, and even some teachers attempted to hide their grins. So I took another guess.

Once again, I was wrong.

More laughter, more sniggering. In fact, at this point, the deputy head leaned into me and asked if I'd like to return to my seat at the back of the hall with the rest of my year group.

Naturally, I refused and took another guess at his card.

'Was this your card, sir?'

'Yes!' he exclaimed.

It wasn't, and I knew that. But he was trying to be nice to me and get me off the hook.

'It wasn't really though, *was* it?' I said, faking some nerves.

'No, it wasn't, but it's ok.'

By now, the energy in the room had changed and there was a sense of palpable embarrassment. And let me tell you – that was exactly the energy I was aiming for. If I have an opportunity to make the audience really feel the embarrassment of the magician, I will. Because that way, when the tension breaks, and the trick is revealed, the pay-off is so much greater.

'But, sir, if this wasn't your card, then what was it?' I asked, feigning desperation.

'The three of clubs, Joel.'

I smiled.

'Ah . . . but you see, that's impossible. You couldn't have chosen the three of clubs – because that card isn't even in this deck! Have a look for yourself.'

The deputy head looked at once confused and sceptical. He took the deck from me and began to rigorously search for the three of clubs. Of course, he came up short. 'It's gone!' he exclaimed.

There was now an excited muttering throughout the hall. Everyone could feel that something amazing was about to happen.

'I'll tell you the truth . . . there was once a three of clubs in that deck. But it's travelled around the room, bounced off of the walls and . . . landed, in your pocket, sir. Take a look.'

He stood still for a second, too nervous to check.

Finally, he reached his hand into his pocket and pulled out . . . nothing.

'Well, that would have been good,' I joked.

Everyone burst into laughter. I was addicted to that feeling. I still am!

'Sir, I want you to follow my instructions as closely as you can. Ok?'

'Ok.'

'I want you to slowly leave this assembly hall and make your way to the staff room. Once there, I want you to check your mailbox. Take out whatever you find and come back to me.'

'You're joking.'

'Am I?' I looked the man dead in the eyes and didn't flinch.

Slowly but surely, the deputy head made his way out of the room. The assembled students stayed silent, awaiting his return.

Moments later, he walked back through the assembly-hall doors, holding one card high above his head.

The three of clubs.

The whole school went crazy. Even the teachers looked at each other in disbelief. And I knew, from that moment onwards, that this was exactly what I wanted to do for the rest of my life.

I can't take *all* the credit for the magic . . . I did have the help of one of the other teachers, who, I hope, kept my secret. But it meant that in primary school, I had a reputation for being the magic kid. And almost everyone respected and appreciated it. I never heard anything negative about what I did, and the teachers were always incredibly supportive.

The same carried through to secondary school. Everyone I knew respected my little hobby. With one exception. One boy. One terrible nuisance. For the purposes of this story, let's call him Ben.

Ben was a tall, broad and good-looking fella – the type of guy who everyone knew, but didn't get that close to. And that was because he was, at the end of the day, a little intimidating. But it's strange, because the whole time I was in school, I never actually realised that he *was* that intimidating.

He was so charming and so funny that his various remarks and backhanded compliments never really seemed that bad. He could make others feel stupid, belittle them, but always in such a way that never once landed him in trouble. He was the type of kid who could spit in a teacher's face and somehow talk his way out of it. A talent? Maybe. Frustrating for everyone around him? Definitely.

And I certainly never realised that *I* was on the receiving end of his behaviour. But I guess I was. At least, I often dreaded any classes in which I was seated near him, and I always felt a sense of having to really focus on not doing something *embarrassing* around him. It was odd, because if you had asked me, I would have told you that Ben was one of my best school mates. He had that sort of you-want-to-be-my-friend vibe, even if he was sometimes nasty. So for the first three years of secondary school, I put up with his ongoing nonsense and manipulation, forever feeling bad about myself around him.

Ben gave me a particularly hard time about the magic. He gave me the nickname 'magic boy'. Classic Ben. It was the sort of nickname that probably wouldn't sound all that offensive if used by the right person, but when *he* said it, you could tell that it was meant as an insult.

He would always try to ruin the magic for everyone by exposing the method of my tricks. Or at least, his version of the method. It was so infuriating because he would often take ridiculous guesses at how a trick was done, yet deliver his message with such confidence that everyone would accept what he said as truth.

And it was clever. Because I would often feel the need to prove him wrong by showing him how the trick actually did work, only to realise that he had been hoping for that the entire time. Smart kid. He knew how to play people.

I think that he held a particular secret dislike for me, probably because I was actually similar to him in many ways: I was charismatic, liked by teachers and one of the only other people who could match him in class tests. The difference being, I wasn't a prick. (I am biased.)

One day, in my third year, we were in an art class – and as everyone who has taken art in third year knows, it's barely a class. Don't get me wrong – art is an incredible subject, but what often ends up happening is that the teachers neglect anyone they think is not going to take it on to GCSE level. And it makes sense – I mean, most people in my class, including myself, were barely capable of potato-print paintings.

So I was sitting in the art room at a table with a small group of friends. One of whom was Ben.

Naturally, I carried a deck of cards (or two, or three) around with me everywhere I went, including school. I spent most of my time in classrooms secretly practising sleight of hand underneath the desk, often getting caught when I dropped all the cards on the floor. It happened more times than I can count.

As such, when classes like art came about, we'd play cards. Usually 'Jack Change It', '21'or, if we were feeling particularly violent, 'Spit'.

I'm a competitive person. I remember being so into a game of spit with my cousin once that I broke her fingernail and it fell off. You see, the thing is, when your entire identity is wrapped up in being 'the magician', and you're bad at practically every

form of competitive game, losing at cards hurts. It was one thing I *should have* been good at.

The annoyance arises when you realise that as a magician, when you win, people assume you've cheated. And if you lose – well, then you're a terrible magician. Either way, you face some sort of negativity.

But back to the art room. We were sitting around the paint-splattered table, playing cards. A normal Wednesday afternoon. But we weren't playing our normal games. This particular afternoon, we'd decided to play something else.

Knuckles.

I had learned it from me dad. He had shown me the game once when I was a kid, and I remember always being too scared to play. Apparently, my dad and my uncle used to practically fight to the death to win.

If you haven't played it, here is how it is done (or, at least, the rules we played by):

- **One deck of cards. Two people.**

- **The deck is shuffled and placed on the table.**

- **One player cuts off any number of cards, lifts the card they cut at and shows it around. Whatever number is on that card is the number of times you get to hit the other player across the knuckles with the entire deck of cards.**

- **The players take turns, until one gives in and admits defeat.**

That probably sounds relatively tame. Let me assure you, though – it's brutal. Barbaric. But about as much fun as two teenagers could hope to have in an art classroom. (Remember, this is before the days when we had iPhones or any other form of portable entertainment. Snake on a Nokia brick was about the best you could get!)

So Knuckles it was. And can you guess who I was playing against? That's right – Ben.

As I said before, Ben was broad. And also very strong. At least, compared to me with my breadstick-like fingers. Which meant it was probably not a good idea to play a fair game against him. So I didn't. I cheated. I know that makes me as bad as him, but trust me – this kid was not going to go easy on me, and I knew it. If I could use anything to my advantage, I was going to.

There's a concept in magic known as 'forcing'. Forcing basically means that you can rig the outcome of a seemingly random decision. For example, you may have heard of 'loaded dice'. These dice allow someone to roll a seemingly random number, but, of course, the dice are slightly weighted, so the magician knows in advance which numbers will show up.

The same can be done with cards, using sleight of hand. There are literally endless ways to force a card, but in the next section I'm going to teach you the one I used when playing Knuckles with Ben. Use this knowledge for good. Or not – it's really up to you.

By forcing the cards, I was able to actively choose the number of times that I would mercilessly crack Ben over the knuckles instead of relying on good fortune. An unfair advantage that I was more than willing to utilise.

Of course, if I was caught, the consequences would be tragic, so I made sure to play in a way that seemed to be fair. I didn't force tens and nines every single time. Instead, I occasionally picked a two or a three, just to avert suspicion. But overall, I got at least twice the number of hits that Ben did.

Nevertheless, when Ben and I had been playing for about thirty minutes, I was getting to the point where, although I was cheating, I was still losing. Ben was just much stronger than I was, and one hit for him was equal to five for me. Fair play.

I was about to give in and call the whole thing quits. My hands were bleeding badly, and I knew that I had a piano lesson after school. Turning up with bleeding hands wasn't exactly my idea of appearing professional to my tutor.

'Honestly, Ben, I think I'm going to have to stop after this round. This is mad,' I laughed.

And that was when he made his mistake. Instead of taking the win, and moving on with his day, Ben decided to lay into me with the most demeaning insult I had ever heard. I can't put it in this book, because it'll offend too many people, but I can promise you that what he said infuriated me so much that I felt all the pain in my hands disappear. He didn't just insult me, but also my brother, who he notoriously picked on, too, whenever he got the chance.

I saw red.

'One last round, then,' I muttered.

He chose a card. It was the king of spades, meaning thirteen hits. Ouch.

One, two, three hits, and I felt my eyes water.

Three, four, five, and I saw the skin on my knuckles shred.

Six, seven, eight, and the pain was searing. But he was playing fair, so I let him keep going.

When he clattered the cards down for one final blow, I bit my lip to stop myself from shrieking. My hand was battered. It looked like I had taken a red-hot iron and rammed it into my knuckles as hard as I could.

My turn.

Ben was watching my hands closely, so I couldn't cheat. He'd have spotted it. Plus, with my hand being so sore, I doubt I would have been able to pull off the move convincingly.

I reached down, cut the deck and chose a card at random. It was an ace. An ace equalled one hit. Great.

I had one shot. One chance to do as much damage as possible. I thought about what Ben had just said, and all the things he had said before. Hiding all the pain behind what I hoped was a composed expression, I took the deck, and held the cards in the best grip I could.

Ben held out his fist. For a brief moment, I thought to myself, Is this really worth it? Why am I even entertaining it? I had almost made up my mind to give in and let him off the hook. Until . . .

'How's it feel to be a loser? Losing at the one thing you're supposed to be good at!'

That was all I needed.

If there's one thing that I will never tolerate being called, it's a loser. Such a simple word, but one that cuts so deep. Call me anything else, and I won't get offended. But a loser? No thanks.

I don't know what came over me, but I somehow brought the cards down with such force that when I hit the back of Ben's hand, I immediately felt something different.

CRACK.

I had broken his knuckles, in one fell swoop.

Being the cool, calm and collected person that he was, Ben didn't immediately react. But I could see in his eyes that he was in extreme pain. For a moment, I felt amazing. Then I felt truly bad.

'I'm so sorry, are you ok?' I spluttered.

'What do you mean? I'm, fine. Another round? Or do you quit?' said Ben, his hand shaking.

'I quit, Ben, you win. Good game.'

His enormous grin and his arrogance instantly made me wish I had hit him harder, but regardless, we wrapped up the game, with about twenty minutes left in the class.

Five minutes went by, and Ben stayed fixed to the spot, not wanting anyone to know his discomfort.

'Are you sure you're ok?'

'I'm fine, Magic Boy.'

Ten minutes. You could see his hand beginning to swell. And then the pain must have reached a tipping point because he suddenly got up, asked to leave for the bathroom and ran out of the classroom.

He didn't come back to the lesson. Instead, he went to the nurse's office, where he said he had hurt his hand 'falling down the art department stairs'. I often wonder whether he made up that lie to keep me out of trouble or to save himself embarrassment. I presume the latter.

Funnily enough, Ben never bothered me again in school. And while we were never close, there seemed to be a sort of new-found respect in his attitude towards me. Over the years, he actually became a pretty nice guy.

So what's the moral of the story? Learn how to force a card? Well, it might prove useful, but no – not quite. Go out and break someone's knuckles to prove a point? No.

What I do suggest is that you never tolerate someone making you feel stupid for going after what you love. Ben was one example of someone who often poked fun at what I enjoyed, or even tried to embarrass me for it. But he wasn't the only one.

I've had teachers, friends, even family members who have subtly tried to drag me down from time to time. Please don't let this happen to you. We can't control what people say or do to us, but we *can* control how we react – although these days, I like to take a slightly less violent approach to settling feuds!

So if someone ever tries to make you doubt yourself, or makes you feel stupid for wanting to pursue your wildest dreams, remember the words of Robert Downey Jr:

'Smile, agree, and then do whatever you were going to do anyway.'

If it works for Iron Man, it works for me. Love you 3000.

FORCE A CARD
(I BROKE HIS KNUCKLES!)

One of the most valuable things to learn when studying magic is a *card force*.

With this one principle alone, you can perform miracles! You can teleport, predict the future, tear and restore cards . . . the possibilities are endless. Like most things in magic, there are countless ways to achieve a force, but I'm going to teach you two. First, I'll show you how I forced cards when playing Knuckles with Ben, and then, I'll show you a way to do it that is so simple it requires no sleight of hand.

Ready? Let's go.

PALM FORCE

This method requires some guts.
It's bold, but it's also very effective.

1.

2.

3.

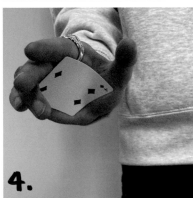

4.

5.

6.

THE TRICK

THE SECRET

Here's how it works:

- Place the cards on the table, squared up neatly and face down.

- Ask the spectator to reach down and pick up as many cards as they want.

- You then reach down and pick up the card that was cut to.

- Little does the spectator know, that the card was forced! But how?

Very simple: the card was *palmed* in your hand the whole time.

Your next question might be: what does 'palmed' mean?

Palming refers to the concealment of an object in your hand – in this case, the card you want – unseen by the spectator. You simply place a card on your hand, with your fingers held in a way that conceals it entirely (see photo 4). By slightly bending your fingers, you can keep the card in place, so that it remains hidden, even when you move your arm.

If you have very small hands, this might be challenging for you. But even then, there are ways around it. Instead of holding the card flat on your hand, you can try bending it and clipping it between your fingers.

When the spectator/opponent lifts up the pack of cards, all you have to do is reach down with the hand that's concealing the forced card and pretend to have picked it up from the pile (see photos 5 and 6). The more you practise this move, the more natural it will seem.

1.

2.

3.

THE TEN—TWENTY FORCE

This force is surefire and so simple you'll be doing it in minutes.

THE TRICK

- Place a deck of cards on the table.
- Ask the spectator to choose a random number between ten and twenty, and silently deal that number of cards from the top of the deck to the table. Close your eyes for this, so there is no way you can see anything.
- Next, ask the spectator to pick up the cards from the table, hold them in their hands and check that they are all different. The spectator confirms that this is the case. Ask the spectator to mentally add together the digits of their randomly chosen number, and to deal down that number of cards to the table. Whichever card they end up on is their randomly chosen card.

But of course, that card isn't random; it was forced. And you can reveal the card in any number of ways.

4.

5.

6.

THE SECRET

Before you hand the deck to the spectator, place the card that you'd like to force nine cards from the top (see photo 1).

That's it. That's all you have to do. Then, no matter which number they choose between ten and twenty, the final card will always be your forced card. Try it for yourself!

Take note of the ninth card from the top, and then deal down any number of cards between ten and twenty. Once you've done that, add the two digits of your number together (for example, sixteen would be 1 + 6 = 7). Now pick up the cards you've already dealt to the table, deal off seven and bingo, you've hit your forced card!

Easy, reliable and mathematically incomprehensible to an arithmetic phobic like me.

7.

HOW TO USE A CARD FORCE

Sure, you now know some card forces. But what good is a card force to you, anyway? Here are some simple things you can use your new trick for – things that will blow the minds of many.

TELEPORTATION

Think about it . . . if you know in advance what card somebody is going to pick, then you can prearrange for that card to be absolutely anywhere, whether that means sneaking a duplicate card into someone's pocket, in an envelope, even across the world, only to be found on FaceTime by a friend – your options are endless!

Place a duplicate card somewhere in advance. Keep the location a secret. Now force the spectator to pick that card using the card force. You can create the illusion that the seemingly chosen card has teleported to the preselected location!

Oh, a little tip. While your spectator is reacting to the teleportation of their *randomly chosen* card, take advantage of that distraction and slip the forced card out of the pack. That way, if they care to check the pack for any gimmicks or gadgets, they won't find their card, adding an extra layer to the illusion.

PREDiCTiON

This is as simple as it sounds (but, in my opinion, not the best way to use a card force – I think it points too clearly to the method). But should you care to, you can place a duplicate card in an envelope, or even simply write the forced card down on a slip of paper before the trick begins. This acts as a prediction. You would require a second pack of cards to do this.

MiND READiNG

I like this. If you can absolutely convince someone that they had a free choice of playing card, then you can absolutely convince them of your ability to read their mind.

Once they've chosen their card and committed it to memory, ask them to keep it a secret. Then, stare into their eyes (try not to fall in love) and announce their choice of card. You'll get crazy reactions to this. It turns the trick from 'I know what card you picked before you picked it – figure that out,' to 'I don't know what card you picked . . . but I'll figure it out!'

Learning how to force a card is an awesome thing to do. Spend some time practising it, and soon you'll have the ultimate party trick!

Growing up with parents who both work in youth ministry, I had the great joy of going away to summer camp with my friends every year from the age of eleven. Those trips remain some of the best days of my life, with endless fun and memories that will last for ever.

Of course, as a teenager, in the midst of *finding myself*, or whatever it is that teenagers do, I relied heavily on being 'the magic guy'. Out of seven summer camps, only once was there ever another teenage magician who rivalled my position as camp prestidigitator (trying to take my 'magic guy' crown).

I used my magic to stand out and, more often than not, to hide any adolescent insecurities I was facing at the time. Acne? Pick a card. Bad at sports? Look . . . a coin from behind your ear!

Most magicians who started young will tell you that they went through the same thing. A lot use magic as a substitute for real confidence. Some, like myself, eventually grow out of this, though I'd argue that most don't. And I understand why. It's incredibly hard to transition from being an exciting, almighty legend who can manipulate reality to being a *normal person*.

At any rate, going through summer camps, I used magic to impress and entertain my friends, as well as the camp leaders. Where most campers' rucksacks were stuffed with clothes, camp merchandise and sweets, mine was packed to the brim with cards, magnets and all sorts of magical gimmicks.

That was until I discovered hypnosis. The moment I realised that I could hypnotise people, it was

game over. Evenings in the guys' cabin were about to reach a new level of mayhem. And no need for any fancy props.

I was seventeen, and it was my last year of summer camp with my friends. But this year, instead of attending as campers, my friends and I volunteered as members of the work crew for the camp. We each had different jobs, from housekeepers to dishwashers.

My role was to clean the dining hall and serve the campers food. It was good fun and, quite frankly, the easiest job. After a day's work on the camp, the work crew would hang out in the den, where we'd eat together, hang out, play games and, most importantly, flirt with each other. Remember, we were teenagers.

On the third night of camp, my services were called upon.

'Joel, can you do some magic for the group?'

I jumped at the opportunity. Truth be told, I'd probably been secretly hoping to be asked. It's worth mentioning that at these camps, there was a mix of teenagers from Northern Ireland, Ireland, Scotland, England and Wales. So I didn't know everyone there, which was even better, giving me more scope for hypnotic success. I'd come a long way since first practising hypnosis and could now do some pretty cool things. I'd stick people's hands together and make them smell things that didn't exist. But more on that later.

I asked the group to sit down and form a circle. Time to get brainwashing. When hypnotising a group it's good to find the best subjects through a series of suggestibility tests. So with the group now sitting in a circle, I began my testing. (I use tests such as 'magnetic hands', 'heavy head' and 'magnetic fingers'.) Among the whole group, I instantly spotted one person who was substantially more suggestible than the rest.

Quite honestly, I had never seen anything like it in my life. Upon giving the command that the group would begin to feel their hands magnetising together, I heard a clapping sound. I flicked my head in the direction of the noise and found myself looking at a boy I didn't know particularly well. I had only met him three days prior, but there he was with his hands touching, the instant that I suggested they would attract each other. I had never seen hypnosis work so quickly.

I'm going to call this guy John. That's not his name, but it'll act as a placeholder. His real name is of no consequence.

'John, I'd like you to stand up for me.'

He did so.

'And notice, that the moment you do, you will not be able to move a muscle. The harder you try to move, the more firmly your entire body will lock into place.'

And it worked. John stood there, motionless, unable to move. I quickly realised that this was the most hypnotically susceptible person I'd ever met. Let the fun begin, I thought.

Thereafter, every single evening, all the guys would get together in the dorm room kitchen, and we'd do hypnosis. Hilariously, John was more keen for this than anyone else, and loved the fact that his suggestibility was entertaining the rest of the group. Such a hero.

As you would expect, every time I would ask John for permission to hypnotise him, I always kept a close eye on him afterwards. You see, sometimes if someone is in trance for too long, they can experience amnesia or even headaches. So his wellbeing was a top priority.

Those evenings involved some of the funniest moments of my life. We were accomplishing things with hypnotism I had certainly read about, but never thought to be actually possible. How about some examples?

Some personal favourites were: making John believe I was invisible, turning everyone in the room into famous football players, changing John's sense of taste, even causing him to genuinely believe that the floor was lava. (A radiator he jumped on to in order to escape the deadly heat fell off the wall.)

Some of this seems far-fetched, I know. But trust me, I was just as blown away by it as everyone else. It seemed borderline impossible that somebody could be that susceptible.

At this point I'd like to come clean and admit that I did pull one rather unpleasant prank on John.

When in trance, I used the command that every single time he shook hands with me, he'd feel the equivalent to a kick in the . . . well, you can probably guess. In addition, he'd have no idea why it was happening. I managed to pull off this little prank up until the last day of camp; his face, as he discovered why this unusual malady had struck him, was priceless. (Of course, let's remember that John didn't experience any real pain – it was all in his mind. Still, a little cruel, perhaps. But funny.)

One evening, after wrapping up our psychological experiments, we decided it was time for bed. It must have been 3 a.m. or so, as was the norm for us. The highlight of that evening had been causing John to believe that we were all speaking French (a language he couldn't speak), and when we hit the hay, exhausted after hours of laughter, little did we know that the next day was about to get very strange.

Waking up early to prepare the tables for breakfast, I made the five-minute journey to the showering blocks. I got ready, and then headed towards the camp centre. Every morning I would stop by the kitchen to say good morning to John, who worked as a dishwasher. He was always first to show up in the mornings, as he had an incredible work ethic.

But John wasn't there. I was sure he had simply slept in – nothing to worry about. All good. So I left the kitchen and went about my morning duties. Breakfast was served as normal, we cleared the tables and then returned to the den to hang out and eat our own breakfast.

'Has anyone seen John?' asked the leader. 'We need the breakfast dishes washed, and he hasn't shown up.' Nobody had seen him. 'I'm sure he's just slept in,' I said. 'He's been working like crazy and has barely slept. I'll go and fetch him.'

So, along with two other guys, I headed towards our dorm. Upon opening John's bedroom door, we were confused. He wasn't there. Nor was he in the bathroom, the kitchen or anywhere else in the cabin.

That was when we started to panic. It wasn't like John to do anything without letting the rest of us know, let alone not show up to his work. He was the hardest-working guy on the camp, so this was majorly out of character.

I had no idea where he could possibly have been. Not wanting to cause alarm, however, the three of us set off to find him. He wasn't in the games room. He wasn't in the office. And yes, we even considered the girls' dorm – but he wasn't there either. We even searched the forest trail, to no avail. Where could he possibly be?

And then, it hit me. It was just a theory, but I had a feeling I knew where John might be. In fact, I was almost certain.

'Follow me!' I exclaimed, as I started to run towards the communal showers. I was convinced that we would find him there. We burst into the showering block, and initially saw nobody. 'John?' I called out.

'Joel? Is that you?'

It was John.

As I expected, there he was, standing underneath the shower, hand gripped around the hot and cold tap. He caught my gaze, and I instantly felt sheepish. I knew what had happened, and it was clear that he did, too.

Throughout the week I had been giving John hypnosis commands that he would later forget. And the night before, I had attempted another one of my little games.

You see, I thought that it would be particularly funny to command John's hand to stick to the bathroom tap the next time he used the bathroom. I also told him that he wouldn't understand why it had happened. The idea being that when he used the bathroom later in the evening, he would find himself stuck and call out for help.

It would have been funny – but the trouble was, having stayed up until 3 a.m., and being teenage boys, we hadn't bothered to use the bathroom. Instead, we'd all gone straight to bed.

John, who was exhausted, had slept in, as I had guessed. He headed straight to the showers, after everyone else had already been, and his hand had instantly glued itself to the shower tap. He had stood there, shouting for someone's attention for hours. But with the shower block being five minutes away, no one had heard him.

All it took was a swift snap of the fingers, and his hand fell loose from the tap. Bless his soul, he wasn't even angry – just hungry and confused. Thankfully, he saw the funny side.

What a guy.

I often wish I could go back to those times . . . so much fun, laughter and irresponsibility. John and I have remained close friends ever since, and sharing an interest in hypnosis, magic and mentalism, we've travelled to see a bunch of magic shows together.

To this very day, I could still call him on the phone and, within thirty seconds, have him sound asleep. Brilliant.

Out of all the stories in this book, this one seems the most far-fetched. But if you ever meet me in person, ask me for John's real name, and I'll gladly put you in touch. He, along with many of my friends, will be happy to confirm the facts.

Utter madness.

Oh, and John, if you're reading this . . .

'SLEEP!'

TRICK TOK

– INTRODUCTION TO THE ULTIMATE GUIDE TO SOCIAL MEDIA SUCCESS

I've been on social media for years, but until my first viral video took off, I'd had no joy whatsoever in getting people to pay attention to me. And the thing was, when 'Magic in Tesco' went viral, I genuinely thought that it was just down to pure luck.

However, looking back, that simply wasn't the case. That video had followed a very specific formula, which I have since used time and time again to help promote myself and others. The only difference is that now I use it on purpose.

For years and years, I dreamed of having a platform where I could share my magic with the world, and now, thanks to social media, that's totally possible. It's possible for me, and it's possible for you, too. So if you have ever wondered what it might take for you to grow a social media platform to a substantial size and you're prepared to put in some work, then you'll definitely get value out of this.

What I'm about to give you are my top pieces of advice when it comes to social media. I tried for years and years to build an audience, with no luck. And I can say, with 100 per cent authenticity, that most of the stuff that you'll hear about how to grow an audience is wrong.

Typically, the people who are spilling information about how to grow a following have never done it themselves, and their theories are mere guesswork. I listened to them for years, and it got me absolutely nowhere. And I'd hate for the same to happen to you.

Of course, this information is totally useless unless applied. I've used these principles to build a social media following of almost 10 million people at the time of writing. Although that number is relatively small in comparison to many other entertainers on the internet, I think there may be some lessons here that will be useful to someone who is starting out; and these ideas are not only for magicians – I've seen them work for dancers, artists and comedians, too.

But before I go any further, I'd like to give a massive thank you to my friend Luca Gallone. He was the first person to be honest with me, and to help me when it came to socials, as well as countless other things. Most of what I'm about to teach you has come from advice he gave me. I certainly wouldn't be writing this book if it wasn't for his invaluable help.

And now, I want to offer you some of the lessons I've learned. So let's go!

TRICK TOK ONE:
THE BASICS

THE KEY TO GROWING AN ACCOUNT ON SOCIAL MEDIA IS TO GET EYEBALLS, AND THEN TO CONVERT THOSE EYEBALLS INTO FOLLOWERS.

SO HOW DO WE DO THAT?

NICHE CONTENT

First, you'll need content. For me, content is video footage of me performing magic tricks. For you, it depends on what your page is going to be about. Which brings me to my first point: pick a niche.

I know, it's a cliché. It's advice I heard for years, but never followed. But you need to niche down. You need to pick something that is going to be the primary focus on your page and go all in.

Why? Well, let's imagine that you follow all the other advice I'm going to give you correctly, but mess this step up. You get a viral video. Millions of people see your piece of content, and because of that, they click on your profile. Perfect, right? You'll get millions of followers, guaranteed. Well, not quite. In some cases, you might get very few. Genuinely. It happened to me.

When I posted 'Magic in Tesco', my page was a mess. Sure, it was titled 'Joel Magician' but there was so much unrelated nonsense there that anyone clicking on it would be put off or confused as to what they'd be setting themselves up to see more of.

I got over 7 million views on that video. But I only gained 15,000 followers. That might seem like a lot, but let's do the maths: only 1 in 466 people decided to follow me after seeing it. Why? Because I hadn't niched down. Compare that to today: I've had videos with far fewer views growing my account to five times that!

So pick a niche, and focus your content around it; mine is magic, but it could be cooking, dancing, comedy, politics, drama, make-up – just about anything.

OTHER KEY POINTS

Now for some other very simple but absolutely compulsory points:

Good lighting These days there are no excuses for bad lighting. Lighting is genuinely more important than camera quality, and you can pick up a ring light for less than the cost of a cup of coffee and a panini in some places. Get one and use it. It doesn't need to be fancy.

Strong profile picture Your picture is the first thing someone will see when they land on your profile, so make sure it's high quality and contrasting (use the contrast tool when editing the photo – you want it to stand out and the extra contrast will create a visual impact; see my profile picture for reference). An up-to-date headshot will do. If you're confused as to what this should look like, just look at any A-list celeb's social media.

Interesting and informative bio Your social media bio (or description) should summarise what you do simply and effectively. Think of it as a business card that you can change for free, as often as you like. Play around with it until you find something that is to the point, catchy and tidy.

All of these things seem super simple, but you'd be amazed how much of an impact they make on converting viewers into followers. So before you move on, make sure they are all in place.

HYPNOSIS
ON THE
BEACH

The legendary Derren Brown has always been my hero, my one true idol. He is, in my opinion, the greatest magic performer of our time.

When I was twelve years old, I had the privilege of seeing him perform his show *Svengali* at the Belfast Waterfront Auditorium. It was my first live magic show experience. And what a way to kick things off.

I truly believe that upon leaving that show, I had the worst headache of my life. And no, I wasn't sick. My mind was just completely blown away by the level of intelligence, creativity, showmanship and overall genius that man can bring to a stage.

Since then, I've seen Derren perform many times. I presume he has no idea who I am (although Derren, if you are reading this, I adore you and hope to buy you dinner, one day).

Not only did *Svengali* include my favourite magic trick of all time (the upside-down painting trick), it also happened to be the first time I had ever witnessed hypnosis live. Up until that point, it was the type of thing I had seen on TV and in movies, but certainly not in the flesh.

Derren stuck a participant's hand to a table, removed the sense of touch from that hand, and even convinced the participant to stick a needle through it. Incredible stuff. I was gobsmacked. And I was hooked.

Upon leaving the theatre, I decided I was going to learn how to hypnotise people. But of course, I was twelve years old and didn't know where to start.

So I did what any other Gen-Z would do. I went to Google. Man's best friend. I found videos, books and old audio recordings from years before, and I began to study. And I came to a conclusion: hypnosis is totally fake.

How did I come to that conclusion? Well, simply because I didn't understand it. If you study old hypnosis books, you'll find that there are lots of methods, but very little explanation as to why it actually works. Perhaps I was looking in the wrong place, studying stage entertainment hypnosis rather than hypnotherapy. At any rate, a lot of the advice was simply, 'Try this out; I guarantee it will work'. No thanks.

And since I couldn't find *the secret*, I was convinced that all the books, seminars and video performances were all crude fakes, designed to confuse the Muggles. Some sort of sick joke. Worse still, I convinced myself that even heroes of mine, like Derren himself, were in on the joke, leading the rest of us mere mortals down the garden path to a field of total nonsense.

It turns out I was wrong. Completely wrong. Hypnosis is real. It's just not what most people think it is.

**But how did I find out?
Simple: I was hypnotised.**

Let me take you back to my first ever job. When I was twelve, I got my first paid gig, performing magic tricks, table to table, at a local cabaret club. (I have all sorts of stories from that job.)

I would usually perform for a couple of hours, doing magic tricks on the guests. But on one special Saturday night, there was a one-off hypnosis show. I don't remember the name of the hypnotist, and perhaps that's for the best, as he was an awfully rude, misogynistic man. Nevertheless, he was an excellent hypnotist.

The cabaret club very kindly invited me to see the show, and I was extremely excited. In my mind, I was about to see definitive proof that this whole hypnosis deal was fake. Derren Brown might get away with it, but not a local charlatan. Clearly, he had brought in some actors to sit in the front row and pretend to be chickens (or whatever else the hypnotist got them to do).

But that's where I was wrong.

The hypnotist stood on stage, made some cringeworthy jokes and eventually got stuck into his set. As is standard in most hypnosis acts, he warmed up with some suggestibility tests to find his ideal participant.

Isn't that convenient, I thought. Of course, he would choose his volunteers, rather than them being selected at random. Proof, I declared to myself, that this man was a fraud.

The hypnotist began to give the audience instructions – to relax, to make our minds a blank canvas, to lock our hands together tightly together. To listen very carefully to the sound of his voice, every single breath we take bringing us deeper and deeper into a state of total relaxation. Every breath we take locking our hands tighter and tighter and tighter, until we find that our hands are totally stuck and cannot be pulled apart.

What a pile of nonsense, I thought to myself, as I began to pull my hands apart.

Except . . . I couldn't. My hands were stuck together. Nothing would separate them – it was as though Super Glue had been poured all over them.

I was in shock. And I was embarrassed. Not only was hypnosis undeniably real, but I was clearly hypnotically suggestible. Ooops.

The hypnotist began to walk around the room to find his perfect subject. When he reached me, I was out of breath, having tried relentlessly to yank my hands apart. I remember trying sheepishly to hide them, but I was inevitably spotted by the hypnotist.

And then, with a powerful snap of his fingers, my hands fell apart, as though nothing had ever happened.

I would have loved to have taken part in the rest of the show, but having realised that I was only twelve years old, the hypnotist rightly made the decision that a hypnotised child brought up on stage, in an eighteen-plus venue perhaps wasn't the brightest idea.

But it didn't matter. I had found what I didn't even know I had been looking for. Proof that hypnosis was as real as the skinny jeans wrapped around my legs.

It was all I needed.

Back at home, I went straight into the books, seminars and anything else I could get my hands on with a fresh understanding and belief that I, too, could hypnotise people. Even though I didn't understand the psychology behind it as I do now, I had the confidence to at least give it a try.

There was one particular part of hypnosis that fascinated me: putting someone to sleep. At one point in my research, I stumbled across a video of Derren Brown putting a stranger to sleep with nothing but a handshake. Mind-blowing, of course. And all while wearing a perfectly tailored suit. (I really should stop with the Derren fanboying.)

I wanted to do it, too. And so I set out to find the technique. Turns out it was pretty easy to find. The real difficulty with hypnosis is building up the confidence to give it a try and not being afraid to fail – which you inevitably will at first. And no matter how good you get, you always run the risk of looking like a moron, and the person being wide awake when they're meant to be asleep.

But the true joy of being young, is being naive. I didn't even consider the possibility of something going wrong, so I approached the whole game with a relentless confidence – something I've found to be very useful in all areas of magic.

After finding and reading all about a technique known as 'the instant handshake induction', I decided that I was ready to give it a go. And where better to do so than at a beach bonfire with all my friends. (Yes, I know you're surprised, but some of us magicians do, in fact, have friends. At least, that's what we tell ourselves.)

It was around 10 p.m., and it was getting dark. The ambience was perfect. I decided that my best target would simply be the mentally *slowest* of the group. The one who typically never handed in their homework. In reality, suggestibility has nothing to do with intelligence. And who was I to judge, anyway? But I was ignorant in my youth; in fact, typically the most creative people are the best hypnotic subjects. But sometimes, ignorance is bliss, and so I decided to go ahead with my weak-minded plan.

I was ready.

I saw my chance, and I went in for the kill. Taking my friend by the hand, I executed the instant handshake induction.

'And, SLEEP!'

It worked. I couldn't believe my eyes. The poor fellow went out like a light. And unluckily for me, he collapsed straight into my arms. I may be an expert when it comes to magic, but let me tell you, at twelve years old, I was no weightlifter. I could barely lift a pillow, let alone another human being. I crumpled under the bulk of this poor soul, and we both fell on to the sand.

I didn't care. I was still so mesmerised by what I had just accomplished. But there was an issue – a very pressing issue – I hadn't considered.

In my haste to learn how I might hypnotise someone, I had never bothered to learn how to un-hypnotise them. You can see the problem with this approach.

So there we were, lying on the sand, one of us fully conscious, the other . . . not so much. And I didn't know what to do. So I did what I thought would be best: nothing.

I sat and waited. And very little happened. He simply lay there, slumped on the sand, as peaceful as can be.

Finally, it dawned on me that I should just do exactly what the cabaret hypnotist did to me. I snapped my fingers, and confidently exclaimed that in three seconds, he would be wide awake, fully ready to enjoy the rest of his night.

I guess I got lucky that first time because my poor technique combined with a lack of knowledge could very well have knocked me off track for years. But as fate had it, I now had a burning desire to get better and better.

I suppose one thing I learned from this, was that sometimes you don't need to know absolutely everything. In fact, if you do wait until you know absolutely everything before taking action, you may never even try. As my friend Dan would say, 'Start small, start simple'.

But most importantly, just start.

Don't let fear of failure stop you from going after what you want. Even if that does mean psychologically knocking a child out cold on a beach. With no back-up plan. And no professional knowledge.

On second thoughts . . . ignore that!

And it worked!
(Thank goodness.)

Funnily enough, he had very little recollection of what had happened, which is very typical when performing hypnosis. It's something I've since learned how to do intentionally, and something that can lead to all sorts of fun.

HEAVY HAND
(HYPNOSIS GONE WRONG)

So you want to be a hypnotist?

Well, I have one question for you: have you got what it takes? Have you got the discipline, the desire, the raw talent, the persistence, the relentlessness required of any mortal being to step into the world of psychological brainwashing?

No? Good. Because as it turns out, getting started in hypnosis is simple. That's right, simple.

Of course, getting to the point where you have a random volunteer waltzing around on stage believing they're a chicken isn't achievable with no effort, but the great news is, there are a bunch of fantastic pseudo-hypnotic tricks that you can easily pull on your friends and family to convince them that you have become a master of the dark arts.

There are a few things that you're going to need in order to pull off this hypnotic stunt. You will need: some tape, scissors, two 1mm neodymium magnets and three hairs from the head of a wild goat.

Once you've got all of those, you can throw them all in the bin. I just wanted to test your commitment . . . and I bet at least one reader went hunting for goat hair.

To do this trick, all that's needed is you and your words. That's the beauty of hypnosis – it's impromptu and incredibly powerful. You will, however, need a willing volunteer.

THE TRICK

Here's what happens:

- You ask your charming volunteer to hold out their hand, stretched out, palm facing up.

- You then ask them to close their eyes, and to imagine that there is a feather resting on their palm.

- A few moments later, you ask them to imagine another feather being placed on their hand, then another, and another and another . . .

- Next, you ask them to imagine that the feathers have instantly disappeared, but in their place, a heavy book has been placed on their hand. Another book is added, then another and another.

- Finally, ask your volunteer to imagine a heavy brick being dropped on to their hand, and to instantly open their eyes. To their amazement, without them even realising, the hand that was outstretched in front of them has dropped significantly towards the floor, as if a real brick has been on put on it. They did not feel their hand move but will swear that they really did feel it getting immensely heavy.

A surreal demonstration for the volunteer, and an even crazier experience for those who are watching with their eyes open.

THE SECRET

There isn't one.

Kidding!

You see, there is a secret and there isn't. The truth is, this really is just psychology, combined with some physiology. The secret is out in the open, but most people miss it.

Let's deal with the physiological aspect first.

If you extend your non-dominant hand in front of you, stretched out to its fullest, and leave it there, it will eventually tire and drop towards the floor. Try it for yourself now, extend your hand for about a minute, and see how much your arm wants to rest.

Of course, it's likely that you will be more successful with this if you choose someone who isn't bulging with muscle, but even then, the psychological aspect of what you're about to do is going to push most people towards the desired end result.

Also, add to this the fact that the volunteer's eyes are closed. Most of us are less spatially aware than we'd like to believe, so the moment you ask someone to close their eyes and concentrate on what you're saying, they'll lose a lot of awareness regarding the position of their hand relative to the floor.

So, how do we add psychology to the mix, so that it's not just two people waiting around for an arm to tire out.

It's simple, and yet it will take a little bit of practice. You see, as I mentioned earlier, a huge element of what makes hypnosis work is confidence. The person taking part in the trick really has to believe what you're saying, so if you go about it in a way that clearly communicates you don't believe in what you're doing, your performance won't be as effective. You don't have to be word perfect – I used to get so caught up in making sure that I never stuttered or took breaks to breathe that I'd panic, and my patter became unconvincing. Just be sure to give it all you've got. Be convincing!

So what do you say in order to make that hand become genuinely heavy?

You ask the volunteer to imagine a light object on their hand, gradually visualising greater and greater weight. Yet again, confidence is key here. When you speak to the spectator, deliver your instructions in a way that suggests you've done this successfully a thousand times. Practise the patter so it's smooth. You'll be shocked at how this works. I've seen people's hands literally drop to the floor when suggesting that a brick is placed on top of them.

If you've got a tough person and their hand isn't moving, don't worry. Just keep the patter going until, inevitably, it will tire and fall.

The best moment is when the person opens their eyes, and you can see the shock manifest across their face. Because 90 per cent of the time, they won't have felt their hand move, and the contrast of where their hand was before and where it ends up is usually enough to crack a massive smile.

The first time you try it, you'll likely be nervous. But if you want proof that it works, close your eyes and deliver the script to yourself. Visualise the heaviness of the books and the brick. If you really play along, you'll shock yourself with the result, as you can quite literally hypnotise yourself. And if that doesn't give you confidence, I don't know what will!

Use this as a demonstration of the power of the human mind, or as a 'betcha' – whatever works for you.

But whatever you do, have fun, and use your new-found ability to manipulate the minds of others for the good. Or utilise hypnosis the way my friend does – to get free burritos. She has life *all* figured out.

HOW I KILLED MY BROTHER

Throughout my magical journey, I've gone through all sorts of phases. The first I remember was my Jay Sankey phase. He's a Canadian close-up magician and the guy was my idol from when I was six, through to around eleven years old. If you haven't seen him, Google him. Wacky as a bag of frogs, but absolutely awesome. I used all his jokes and tricks – but I never copied his hairstyle.

The same can't be said for my Colin Cloud phase. I had the hair, the coat, everything. This phase lasted from around seventeen to twenty years old. I have nothing but mad respect and love for Colin (he knows how much I adore him and his work). His Edinburgh Fringe shows are still the best mentalism performances I've seen live.

And let's not forget the Derren Brown phase, which is ongoing. I learned very quickly that nobody should even attempt to emulate that man. He's in a league of his own.

It wasn't until around the age of twenty-one that I finally entered the phase I'm in now: the Joel phase. The one where I finally embraced my own style and character, warts and all. My advice to young magicians is to get to this phase as quickly as possible. If it weren't for Colin's very sound advice, to simply be myself, I very likely wouldn't be writing this book.

There are plenty more micro phases that I went through: the Dynamo phase, the Calen Morelli phase, even the Teller phase. Yes, I once had a silent stage act. I can barely keep my mouth shut at the best of times, so I don't know why I ever even attempted to do so in front of a crowd.

However, there was one other magical phase that I haven't yet mentioned. The era of Criss Angel, which started when I was six or seven. I still remember vividly the Christmas morning when I **unwrapped a surprise from my parents. It was Criss Angel *Mindfreak* S2 the box set. I had no idea what I was in for.**

If you've never seen or heard of Criss, I implore you to take a moment and look him up. I'd imagine you'll either love him or absolutely hate him. He's that type of performer. I loved him, and still do. I think, all in all, he's probably my favourite magician/manipulator of reality as we know it.

The theme song for his television series *Mindfreak* alone is enough to convince you to watch the entire thing. Not to mention that he was doing things I had never even dreamed of. Whether levitating over a building or tearing a human being in half . . . the guy was impressive. I was hooked on his material and wanted nothing more on planet Earth than to be just like him. Which was very evident to everyone around me – I got the hat, the shades, the chains. I even convinced my poor mother to buy me a fake-diamond-encrusted Ace of Spades belt. Classy.

Say what you want, but I *was* Criss Angel. At least, I was a watered-down, five-foot-tall version of him, still holding a little puppy fat, as opposed to his washboard abs. (I still don't have the abs, but a man can dream.)

At any rate, I loved the guy. I loved his magic, his style, his attitude, everything. And as such, I began to emulate every trick I saw him do. Quite clearly, I wasn't in a position to levitate over buildings – although I do remember Photoshopping myself soaring above one of our neighbourhood lampposts. My friends weren't quite convinced. But look at me now, haters! Ah, no, I still haven't managed it.

Anyway, let me take you back to one of my fondest childhood memories. The middle of winter on a rainy Sunday afternoon. As you may recall, I had begun to put a little magic show together at quite a young age. This story is set around that time. My shows were a messy, experimental mash of Criss Angel, Jay Sankey, Greg Wilson, Mismag822 (those who know, know) and all sorts of other influences.

Looking back, my poor family had a lot to put up with. I was *that child*: the one who would organise household talent shows (usually a poor excuse for me to do magic) in addition to, well, magic shows. And this was something that I enforced almost weekly. What an obnoxious little show-off. The shows did get better as I got older, eventually turning into shows for the public, but my amazing family would almost always sit politely and watch in those early days.

On one particular Sunday, I remember feeling especially influenced by one of Criss Angel's signature illusions: sawing a woman in half. I decided that this would be the finale to my Sunday-afternoon extravaganza.

Problem: Criss's illusion makes use of a gigantic industrial saw and I didn't happen to have one handy.

Second problem: I didn't have a beautiful assistant to cut in half. What a shame.

But these were minor issues – mere bumps in the road that I would easily overcome on my path to living-room notoriety. No industrial saw? No problem – I had a hammer. No assistant? No problem – I had a brother.

And I still do. Miracuously, he's still in one piece after all the absurd practical jokes and tricks I've played on him over the years. In fact, let me tell you about my brother, Ethan. He is my best friend in the world (at the time of writing, at least – don't mess this up, Ethan) and the one person who has always had my back, through thick and thin. He is two years my junior and the two of us have always been close. Even more so over recent years. If you've ever watched any of my viral social media videos, Ethan is probably in it. Or behind the camera. He's somewhere, to be sure.

Me and Ethan posing for our primary school photograph. Wish I was that adorable now . . .

But let's talk about the stunt of the century. My finest Sunday Magic Show to date.

Usually, these magic shows would take place in our living room, with my parents sat on the comfiest sofa, watching (and probably trying not to giggle at) my latest magical discoveries. They would range from five minutes to a full-blown hour, depending on how much energy I had to spare, based on the sugar I had consumed during Sunday dessert.

I remember preparing for hours and hours, neatly arranging my props on a tiny coffee table before each show. In fact, one of the defining moments of my life was being told by my dearest nana that she recognised my ability to neatly arrange a show as being a real talent. Whether she meant it or not, the comment made me feel so proud of my little hobby, that I kept it up for years. Thanks, Nana.

However, this particular show was unlike the rest. A different beast altogether. Fuelled by inspiration from the Mindfreak himself, I was going to shock and amaze my parents with a classic feat of magic: sawing someone in half. All done with absolutely no consideration for health and safety, of course.

I got to work, and quickly planned out a way to perform this illusion, making use of the furniture and household items available to me. All I needed was a duvet, some pillows, a bicycle helmet, the piano stool, a very real hammer and, most importantly, Ethan.

I placed the piano stool a couple of feet away from the sofa where my parents would soon be seated and placed the duvet on top of it. I instructed Ethan on what he had to do to make the illusion work, and I was ready to go.

The normal Sunday afternoon routine began, with me passive-aggressively inviting my parents to join me in the living room for an amazing, life-changing magic experience. No tickets required – they could just pay with love and admiration.

The lights went down (I turned off the big lamp) and I took centre stage (the carpet). I performed some new card tricks, which intrigued and amazed my parents and definitely *didn't* bore them to tears as you might think.

Then came the time for the big event. The finale. The illusion of a lifetime.

'Ethan!' I exclaimed. 'Please lie upon the bench of wonder and mystery.' (The piano stool.)

Ethan did as he was instructed, and lay down on the piano stool, acting as though he had no idea as to what might happen next.

'I will now cover my random volunteer with this duvet,' I explained (Ethan wasn't chosen at random, of course, but he certainly was – and still is – random), wrapping him completely, like a mummy.

My parents could see the outline of Ethan's body inside the duvet, and not having watched Criss Angel S2 themselves, didn't know what to expect next . . .

SLAM!

In a moment of total violence, I brought down a full-sized hammer upon Ethan's torso. Moving like lighting, I quickly followed up with another painful blow, smashing down on Ethan's cranium. My parents both leapt from the sofa and hurled the duvet off Ethan's limp body in a whirlwind of action, swear words and total shock.

I grinned.

For Ethan wasn't under the duvet.

He was gone. Vanished.

Until . . .

Tap, tap, tap.

My parents turned to the window behind the sofa so quickly that I'm amazed their heads didn't completely fall off!

There he was. Ethan. My younger brother, friend – and now household superstar.

He was standing outside, drenched in the pouring rain, looking in at us with a look of absolute glee.

We had done it.

Our very own Criss Angel illusion, and all in our very own living room.

So how did we do it?

Well, have a look back at the list of required props and you can probably piece it together for yourself. Truth be told, it wasn't difficult to do and it certainly isn't difficult to figure out. But something I've learned over the years is that the reason why most magic fools people is because they don't know what's coming next. That's why you should never perform the same trick twice – a massive hurdle to overcome in this new age of social media magic.

At any rate, the vanishing and reappearance of my younger brother was so unexpected that for a brief moment, as they later admitted, my poor parents thought I had genuinely and mercilessly attempted to assault him.

What a thrill.

Ever since that event, Ethan and I have always worked together on new illusions, funny practical jokes and borderline dangerous stunts. From attempting to catch nerf bullets edged with needles (don't ask) to swallowing swords, we've always had a blast coming up with new and interesting ways to entertain. Except that now, it's no longer in our parents' living room. Now, we have millions of people watching. And I'll never stop being grateful for that.

THIS LITTLE FORMULA WAS A GAME
CHANGER FOR ME. BEFORE I HAD IT,
I WAS STUCK AT AROUND 25K TOTAL
SOCIAL MEDIA FOLLOWERS.
ONCE I GOT IT, I SKYROCKETED TO
10M IN JUST OVER TWO YEARS.
IT'S DECEPTIVELY SIMPLE . . .
BUT IT WORKS. ARE YOU READY?

STEP ONE: HOOK

STEP TWO: BUILD-UP

STEP THREE: REVEAL

LET'S TAKE A LOOK AT EACH STEP
INDIVIDUALLY.

So what do I mean by 'hook'? Put simply, the hook is the very first part of your video – the part that is going to make somebody stop and pay attention to you.

You see, you could have the best video in the world, but if nobody watches past the first three seconds of it, they're never going to find that out. A lot of social media gurus will tell you that you've got about three seconds to capture someone's attention, and while that may have been true a few years ago, it's not any more. Now, you've got just one second to reel them in.

Rightly or wrongly, we do judge a book by its cover. So think of the hook to your video as the cover. If you have a fantastic piece of content, then you owe it to yourself and your potential viewers to use every single trick and tactic possible to get them to pay attention.

But how do you create a good hook? Well, it depends on what your video is about, but here are some good ideas and tips to get you started.

ASK A QUESTION

I use this all the time, and it works wonders for me. When working on a series of videos based around optical illusions, I will capture the audience's attention by saying something like: 'Can you see what's wrong with this image?' Just asking a question is enough to get someone to stop for a brief moment, consider the question and then possibly stick around to discover what the answer is.

USE INTERESTING IMAGERY

This one relates to all niches, but it's particularly suited to magic. If I'm going to perform a magic trick using an interesting prop, you'd better believe that I'm going to hold that prop front and centre. I want the viewer to be subconsciously asking themselves the question: 'What is he about to do with that?' The same principle is applied across all types of content. For example, a dancer may hold an interesting pose at the start of a video or even wear clothing that stands out a mile off.

MAKE THEM WAIT

In a bunch of my videos and videos that have performed very well for others, we'll build an initial image that suggests that something is about to happen, but make the viewer wait for the chaos. The human brain hates unfinished patterns, and we can use that to our advantage. An example in my videos might be where I'm holding a prop in my hand with a red circle drawn in around it. The viewer will likely be curious as to what's about to happen to the prop and wait around to find out.

As an example, which of these two hooks is more likely to get someone's attention?

A man swimming

Or

A man standing on the edge of a pool, just about to dive in.

The man standing by the edge of the pool is more likely to grab someone's interest, making them want to wait to see if anything interesting happens. (Ideally, something interesting *does* happen – otherwise you've wasted their time!)

MAKE A PROMISE

I love this one. It's something I use all the time in my videos.

At the beginning of a video, I'll make a promise/claim – for example, 'I'm about to read your mind in fifteen seconds' or, 'This playing card is about to transform', or even, 'Ethan, I'm about to steal your watch, and you're not going to catch me'.

A statement like this is enough to capture someone's attention and, better still, their curiosity. And if you can make somebody feel genuine curiosity, you'll win this game.

This applies to every single niche. I've seen it done especially well in the personal development space. A video may begin with the guru saying, 'I'm about to give you the number-one piece of advice that changed my life'. Here, by making the promise first, they have hooked the viewer, not only increasing the amount of time that they spend watching the video (and this is important), but also building a sense of trust: the viewer is intrigued and then gets what they've been promised.

CHALLENGE THE VIEWER

Another personal favourite. For this type of hook, you're going to dare the viewer or, even better, tell them they can't do what you're about to suggest.

For example: 'I'm about to fool you with this magic trick, and even if you watch this video back in slow motion, you still won't be able to catch me.'

Listen – I'm not actually arrogant enough to believe that nobody on planet Earth will understand how my magic tricks are done. However, experience has taught me that a statement like that will force the average person to keep watching, just to demonstrate to themselves that they can prove me wrong! The inherently competitive nature of your viewer will ignite, and you'll have snatched their attention in no time.

This hook can be used in lots of different ways. A chef might say, 'You've been making pasta wrong your entire life', while a fitness influencer might say, 'I guarantee I can do ten push-ups in the time it takes you to do three'. That sort of thing. Don't make false claims intentionally though – always try to back up what you're saying, but use people's competitive natures to your advantage.

THE BEST TILL LAST

This one is pretty self-explanatory: you start your video by promising that the best part comes right at the end.

In my case, I may say, 'This illusion is going to blow your mind. But if you watch right until the end, I'll show you how it's done.'

It's a simple tactic that, again, increases overall watch time and creates that 'worth-the-wait' feeling that you want to instill in your viewer. And of course, you do need to deliver.

CUT TO THE CHASE

This one is important and applies to all the above-mentioned hooks. Cut to the chase.

I've seen people use incredible hooks but only five seconds into the video. By that point, the viewer is gone, never to be seen again. So use hooks quickly, boldly and with confidence.

Before filming, ask yourself: how can I make this hook faster? This doesn't necessarily mean saying the words more quickly (although that can help), but ruthlessly slicing the useless filler and nonsense we so often feel the need to add to our content. A lot of the time, things that we find amusing or interesting will just be an excuse for the dopamine-addicted viewer to swipe onwards. So cut the fat in your hook and get to the point immediately. Remember, you have one second to get their attention. Make it count.

A good exercise is to scroll through social media. Any time that you stop on a piece of content, take a moment and ask yourself: what made me do that? What made me stop and take time out of my day to consume this person's idea. You'll find that 99 per cent of the time, there will have been a clever hook, whether it was intentional or not. Take notes on those hooks and make use of the format yourself.

Let me be clear: I'm not saying that you should copy somebody else's idea. Not at all. Rather, have a look at the psychology behind what they've done, and find a way to adapt and implement it into your own personal content.

Also, remember that being fancy doesn't necessarily mean being good. I have friends who have wanted to start social media for years but haven't done so because they 'haven't got an editor' or their 'video isn't perfect'.

I started with an iPhone 6 camera, which at the time of writing, has a camera quality comparable to that of a microwave. In other words, completely useless. As I said before, camera quality is less important than lighting, so buy a cheap ring light and stop making excuses! You've got this.

If you're curious as to how I use hooks personally, I'd encourage you to take a serious look at my videos. I am by no means the best at this, but I do put a lot of time and effort into making sure that I give myself the best possible chance at getting someone's attention.

STEP TWO:
BUILD-UP

DEAD TIME

So you've got your viewer's attention. What now?

Well, it would be a pretty good idea to keep that attention, since you've worked so hard to get it. But how? Well, truth be told, it's easier than getting them engaged in the first place. The key with the middle section of your piece of content is to build to excitement for the reveal at the end.

Once a viewer has made the mental decision to watch past the first few moments, that commitment should buy you some time. Unless of course, you make this fatal mistake . . .

There's a big difference between building excitement and being boring. Just because you've got someone's attention, that doesn't mean you can't lose it. Remember, we're still dealing with people who have painfully low attention spans and are looking for any excuse to impulsively scroll to the next piece of content. As such, you need to make sure that there is no dead time, which is, simply put, time spent on things that don't move the video forward or provide some sort of entertainment or education.

If you're an entertainer, you'll get this right away. We all know that you can lose an audience in an instant, and it can be a pain to regain their attention. The way to counter that, is to give them no excuse to be bored. For me, that means absolutely no time spent saying or doing anything that isn't important or relevant.

Have a look at my content or, for that matter, the content of any creator who has a fairly big social media presence. I guarantee you'll struggle to find a moment in their short-form content that doesn't serve a purpose and keep the video moving.

My general rule of thumb is that something new must happen every three seconds. If three seconds have gone by, and you haven't introduced some new development into the mix, then you will likely lose the viewer. It's harsh, but it's the reality. Even something as simple as a quick zoom in or out is enough to keep the viewer's mind guessing and so keep them engaged.

If you're really entertaining, insightful and a good communicator, maybe you can get away with a one-take wonder with zero edits. If that's you, amazing. If not, take advantage of planning and editing.

Practically speaking, this might mean using editing software to cut out silences, useless dialogue or meaningless movements. It might mean refilming a whole video again, just to reword something. And although this might seem like a lot of work, it's work that pays back tenfold. Most people won't bother. You should.

A WORD ABOUT WATCH TIME

I mentioned earlier that watch time is important.

But what is it? Very simply, watch time is the amount of time someone spends on your piece of content. So if I put out a video that is ten seconds long, and the average watch time is eight seconds, then I've got 80 per cent watch time.

You want that number to be as high as possible. Ideally, it would be above 100 per cent, meaning the viewer has rewatched the video.

So why do we want high watch time? Well, there are two reasons.

Firstly, if your watch time is good, it's an indicator that your content is great. Why would you shoot for anything else?

Secondly, it's what every platform wants. If you can show a social media platform that you're capable of keeping a viewer on their app for longer, they'll reward you for it, via exposure to the main feed. Why? Well, because the platform needs to keep people on the app, or else they can't advertise to them. And if they can't do that, they can't make money. So if you can help the platform by keeping your audience on

the app for as long as possible, then you'll be rewarded with new traffic for you to convert into fans.

Simple? I think so!

Using your video analytics is a great way to help you figure out what you're doing wrong. People typically use analytics to see how many comments, likes or shares they've received, but in my opinion, the most useful form of data is the average watch time.

You can check your average watch time on content on most platforms. If you're not sure how, then just Google it. It's super simple, and very useful. But why?

It's useful because if you can see the average watch time, you'll get a really good idea of why a piece of content has or hasn't done well. Let me explain . . .

Let's say you have a video that is twenty seconds long. It doesn't perform well. And that's ok, as long as you learn from it. So you check the analytics on that post.

Among all the other data, you can see that the average watch time is eight seconds. Now, most people seeing that stat would simply get discouraged and either give up or film a new video.

That's not what you need to do.

Instead, you need to actually use the analytics to find out why people didn't watch past eight seconds. See where I'm going with this?

When you look at the twenty-second video, you pay attention to exactly what happens at the eight-second mark. Usually, there will be something at that precise moment, that's enough to discourage people from viewing any further. It could be a glitch in audio, dead time, bad lighting at that moment, a badly phrased sentence or any number of things. But the key is to identify and take note of it. And make sure not to do it again!

Let me give you a personal example. I posted a video which, based on previous experience, should have reached millions of people. But it didn't. It performed horribly. So I had a look at the analytics.

Turns out, people stopped watching around nine seconds into the video. And I instantly understood why it hadn't performed well – because at the nine-second mark, I used a phrase that *sounded* like a really explicit swear word. I wasn't saying that word at all, but in my Northern Irish accent, some viewers had mistaken what I had said, taken offence and scrolled. This wrecked the watch-time percentage and dragged down my views.

Is the lesson to be learned here that I ought to speak more clearly? Well, kind of, but not really. The key lesson is that I would never have known why the post hadn't performed well if I hadn't investigated and uncovered that watch-time data.

Lucky for you, that data is available, so make sure you use it. If you're going to use stats to improve your videos, at least use stats that are accurate and not the opinions of other people. The numbers don't lie, so be sure to spend time using your data to improve what you do.

Again, this sounds like a lot of work, but it isn't really. Plus, it'll save you a lot of time and pain, trying to do it the hard way.

So all in all, cut the fat, keep things moving – and when things don't work out, check the data to find out why.

So you've got the audience's attention and managed to keep hold of it. Next, it's time to end the video. And, in my opinion, the best way to do that is with some sort of big reveal.

Sure, Joel, you're probably thinking – that's easy for you to do, you're a magician! (I mean, after all, the reveal is a key part of any trick.) But this doesn't just apply to magicians. It applies to anything social-media-related.

So what is a reveal? Well, it could be any number of things. For me, it's usually the magical moment of my trick. For a chef, it might be the unveiling of a dish. For a comedian, it would be the punchline. And you want your reveal to come at the end. I mean – where else would you put it? Otherwise, you would be keeping people around purely to waste their time.

The reveal should be simple for you. All your energy and thought should have gone into the hook and the build-up, so that the reveal is easy.

I'd advise that the moment you've done the reveal, you try to wrap the video up as quickly as possible. Remember, you want that 100 per cent+ watch time, so the longer you keep waffling on after the peak of your video, the greater the chance that your viewer will scroll and not complete it. Better to do the reveal, and then instantly cut the video, so it loops again. That way, you're also ensuring a good rewatch rate.

There's not a lot to say about the reveal besides do it the best you can. The same rules apply to the reveal as to the hook and build-up: make sure you keep things moving and cut the fat.

And that, my friends, is the three-step formula. I hope you make good use of it.

MY FAVOURITE MAGIC TRICKS

Almost every single time I perform a magic trick, whether online or in person, I'm asked the same question: 'What's your best trick?'

And the answer is simple: I don't know! (Some have argued that my best trick is in styling my ferociously curly hair to look as unforgivable as possible.) I don't have *one best* magic trick because my favourite changes on almost a daily basis. That's part of the fun of magic. New methods are constantly being innovated, and new performers bring new styles. It's a fascinating world.

But although I can't tell you what my *best* trick is, I can tell you about the *first* magic trick I ever saw. I remember it so vividly that I sometimes wonder how it was possible for me to have been only five years old. It was an event that drastically influenced the direction of my life.

I was on holiday with my family in Florida: me, Mum and Dad, my brother, Ethan, my sister, Emma, and Nana and Papa. The whole squad.

Me, Ethan, Lucy, Emma, Mum and Dad on hols!

Despite likely being exhausted after a day of madness at Disney World, we all took an evening stroll through Downtown Disney. Anyone who has been there will know that there is no shortage of things to do. It's a real shock to the senses.

Walking alongside my Papa, I noticed his gaze lock on to a little shop that seemed to be less busy than the rest. The words 'Magic Masters' glowed in a bright neon green above its entrance. The store was literally topped off by a 10-foot-tall magician's top hat and wand.

MAGIC MASTERS

I didn't know it then, but my Papa loved magic. He always enjoyed watching Paul Daniels on TV, along with Tommy Cooper and a host of other old-school conjurers. So taking me by the hand, he led me towards the entrance of the magic emporium.

I had no idea what this shop could possibly be. Magic? I hadn't even heard of it. Having never been exposed to a magician on TV, in person or anywhere at all, I had no clue as to what I was about to experience.

The store was small and dimly lit, but utterly enchanting. Countless pieces of magical memorabilia hung on the walls; there was even a replica of Harry Houdini's water-torture cell.

Behind an old mahogany counter stood a man. He was the first magician I had ever seen. A slim, sharp-looking fellow, with long, skinny fingers. I watched the man closely, as he addressed a small group of people standing by the counter. Being only five years old, I was so short that I could barely see over the top. Nevertheless, I stood firmly on my tiptoes and gave the spectacle my full, undivided attention.

The man was standing with his hand outstretched, a little red sponge ball resting on his palm. Upon his command, the ball began to float. Higher and higher, until it stopped in mid-air, then slowly returned to its original position.

I was gobsmacked.

I was experiencing something that was to me, at the time, completely impossible. Every assumption I had made about how the world worked, crumbled before me. My mind began racing with theories as to how to accomplish this miraculous feat. Maybe it was a matter of concentrating all my energy on to the little ball? Or maybe I needed to develop a psychic ability? That must be it, I thought to myself.

In an instant, I made the decision that one day, I would be able to do that, too. If it meant sleepless nights, fine. If it meant failing a thousand times, fine. Even if it meant running through a brick wall – I would learn how to levitate an object.

But as it turned out, there was no need for any of that. Because, for a mere $13.99, the solution could be handed to me on a silver platter. You see, I hadn't understood the fact that I was able to simply *buy* the trick. Or even that there was a trick. To me, what that magician was doing was real. In my eyes, he possessed a rare and unique ability – which in a way, I guess, he did.

Sadly, the $13.99 levitating-ball trick was out of stock, so I didn't get the opportunity to learn it. However, that was only the first of many illusions that I would witness, as what should have been a five-minute trip to a Downtown Disney shop turned into hours and hours in Magic Masters. Papa and I stood in amazement as the magician demonstrated illusion after illusion, baffling us completely.

Finally, after an evening jam packed with magic, we left – and not empty handed. Papa kindly purchased two illusions for me to try out myself, asking me to show them to him once I had mastered the tricks.

Papa never really cared how the tricks were done. For him, the sheer joy of the magic itself was enough. I, on the other hand, need to know how everything works. If, at any point during my life, I've been fooled by a magic trick, I will do anything to discover the method.

And I mean *anything*. I've spent hours and hours at a time, picking apart ten-second increments of magic recordings, just to understand one tiny portion of the method. Magical theory and method became my obsession, and they still are.

At any rate, I left Magic Masters with a smile on my face, ready to race back to the hotel to practise my new magic. I didn't care to see the rest of Disney. This was too important.

The two tricks were the rising card and the pen through the bill. Both fantastic illusions. The rising card trick didn't take much work; thanks to the help of a specially supplied deck of cards, the magic essentially worked itself. The pen through the bill was a little more challenging, but with a few hours of practice, I finally got the move down. Thank goodness that magic instructions come with illustrations, because I certainly wouldn't have been able to understand the method based on text alone – even with my mum reading the instructions for me. Remember, I was five.

My Papa...

the big interview

Meet Joel M. He knows your pin number and can unlock your phone

As requested, I summoned Papa to show him the illusions. Abracadabra, the card rose and the bill was restored. But the real magic was the feeling I got from doing the tricks. Watching someone else doing the magic was one thing, but doing it myself? Forget about it. It was next level.

I still have the card that Papa chose when I performed my first trick. The six of spades. It's one of my most cherished possessions. And to this day, he's still the first to show up to my shows, along with my Nana, who I love so dearly.

My mum and dad will likely be appalled when they hear this, but I don't remember anything else about my trip to Disney. Just the magic. That's how intensely obsessed I was with my new-found discovery. From that moment in the shop onwards, I've never looked back. I've never given it up, and my love for magic has never faded. I'm as passionate about it now as I was then, if not more so.

I think we all have moments in our life that dramatically impact the choices we make, and the things we strive for. I often wonder what would have happened had I not walked into that little magic shop. Where would I be now? Would I ever have taken up magic? Or would I have gone on to be the world's best pole dancer instead? (Apologies for that disturbing mental image.) No one can answer these questions, but it's safe to say that I'm incredibly grateful that events took place in such a way that allowed me to discover magic. It's been the greatest gift I could ever have asked for.

Although I will always remember that first experience as absolutely jaw dropping, there have been many other similar moments over the years since then. I've described how I'd spend every waking second trying to figure out how a trick was done, but there have been times where I've been so clueless, so flabbergasted, so utterly fooled by an illusion, that I've been unable to do anything but momentarily bask in the glory of the performer. As such, I'd love to dedicate the next portion of this book to some of my favourite magicians of all time. Without these people and their work, the world of magic would be a different place altogether. Only a couple of them even know who I am, but they've all impacted me in more ways than they could possibly know.

So without further ado, here are my top picks for the best magical performances I've ever seen. (I should add that the titles of the tricks are very much made up by me – I do hope that's OK, idols of mine.)

CRISS ANGEL: LEVITATION

Of all the tricks I'm about to describe, Criss Angel's levitation illusions are the ones that kept me up at night the most.

On my first viewing of Criss Angel *Mindfreak*, I nearly jumped out of my skin. In broad daylight, Criss levitated from one building to another. I don't know what else to say – that trick alone would be enough to start a religion!

Filmed over fifteen years ago, it still holds up today. Every human being has wondered what it would feel like to fly, but Criss has actually done it, time and time again. He's even vanished in mid-air, out in the open. Ridiculous.

Criss is a prime example of a magician who isn't scared to think big and try things that others have never ever dreamed of. Such an inspiration to me, and many more. MINDFREAK.

DERREN BROWN: THE PAINTING TRICK

As I said earlier, Derren is my favourite magic performer. I honestly can't see anyone else claiming his throne. Many of you will have watched his phenomenal television shows over the years, especially if you're here in the UK. If you haven't heard of him, put down this book, watch him and then come back.

You're welcome.

But here's the thing. If you haven't seen Derren live, you haven't seen him. He's remarkable. A true showman. I've had the luxury of seeing him perform live at least seven times now, and every single time he's received multiple standing ovations. Whenever I leave one of his shows, I feel privileged to have spent time in the same room as him.

Each of his stage shows is fantastic, with my personal favourite being Derren Brown: Secret. But for me, one trick stands out above the rest. It's the painting trick, and it is one of my all-time favourites.

When I saw the trick live for the first time, I hadn't been warned. My brain was knocked out of place so hard that I couldn't think straight for about a week. My eyeballs practically popped out of my skull and hung by the optic nerve. Pure genius, unadulterated talent, short and simple.

But I'm not going to tell you what happens. So if you haven't seen it, you must.

DYNAMO: TIME TRAVEL

Dynamo is awesome. He's a household name, and for good reason. Despite massive adversity, he's built an entertainment empire and has been an inspiration to magicians all over the world.

He's done crazy things; far too many to mention. However, there is one particular trick that I had the joy of seeing live and which instantly became one of my favourites . . . and not for the reason you may be thinking.

Dynamo was performing live in the SSE Arena, Belfast. And of course, I had tickets, bought for me as a Valentine's present by my girlfriend, LB. I was incredibly excited – after all, it's rare that a magician performs in a big theatre, let alone a massive stadium.

What a show! Dynamo killed it. The crowd went wild when he demonstrated illusions that many thought were only possible on TV. He put a borrowed phone in a bottle, levitated and even made a DeLorean car appear! But my favourite trick in the show was the time-travel effect.

Dynamo stood in a single spotlight and held a box full of handwritten notes from the audience in his arms. Suddenly, the notes erupted from the box, flew around his body and, when they fell to the ground, Dynamo had disappeared into thin air.

A split second later, he reappeared at the back of the stadium. Wow. Call it time travel, call it teleportation – all I know is that it was absolutely awesome.

The reason I've chosen this trick as one of my favourites isn't because of the illusion itself. Rather, it was the reaction of my girlfriend, LB, that made the trick a masterpiece for me. Lucy and I have been together for eight years now, and she's seen every magic trick under the sun. Having helped me with my magic shows for years, it's extremely rare for her to be fooled by a magician. But when Dynamo teleported from one side of the stadium to the other, her jaw hit the floor. She admitted afterwards that she wasn't only amazed, but genuinely frightened by how impossible the trick was. It was a visceral shock to the senses.

Bravo, Dynamo, and thanks for making magic cool again.

COLIN CLOUD: EVERYTHING

I can admit when I'm a fanboy. And when it comes to Colin Cloud, a fanboy I am. Not only is he a lovely human being, kind and funny, he is also mesmerising on stage.

I don't have a particular trick in mind here, but if you don't know Colin's work, go and check it out. All I'll say is, prepare to be genuinely frustrated when you can't explain a single one of his demonstrations. He's just too good.

Thanks for all your support over the years, friend.

DAVID BLAINE: WATER TANK

I've always been a massive fan of David Blaine. From his street magic to his death-defying stunts, he never fails to evolve and take his magic to the next level.

In recent years, Blaine's level of insanity has scaled new heights and, luckily for us, he also decided to bring his skills to the stage. I had the pleasure of watching him live in Dublin for an evening I'll never forget.

Along with many other fantastic feats of magic, including sewing his mouth shut with a needle and thread or putting out a fire with water from his stomach (yes, you read that correctly), David performed his world-famous water-tank demonstration.

It's pretty simple. Blaine jumps into a tank of water and doesn't come out for over fifteen minutes. The impressive part being that he's holding his breath the whole time.

I'm going to be completely honest here: I genuinely have no clue as to whether this is real or a devious trick. The magician inside of me wants to believe that there's a clever mechanism at work, but my gut tells me that he's just incredibly disciplined and can do it for real. Either way, it's enthralling.

To my great joy, I was asked to come on stage to inspect the tank while David was under water. It led to me meeting one of my childhood idols – but not exactly under the circumstances I would have imagined.

Imagine reading this entire chapter without taking a single breath. David Blaine could do that. Is it real, or is it magic? We'll never know.

Selfie with David Blaine...

So there you have it. Some of my favourite illusions and my favourite performers. If you get the chance to see any of them live, make sure you do so.

Thank you for inspiring me, and so many others.

RISING CARD
(MY FIRST TRICK)

Ok, this trick is special to me. I really considered not teaching it because it's just so good! Put the work in, and you'll floor people with this little miracle.

The method to the rising card that I was given aged five consisted of magnets, wires, tape and all sorts of ridiculous complications. The version I'm going to teach you here can be easily achieved with nothing but your wits and a normal deck of cards. So . . . what are you waiting for? Grab some cards and get ready to learn an illusion that will melt the minds of all who witness it.

THE TRICK

Here's what happens:

- You show the audience a deck of playing cards, giving them a thorough shuffle, so they can clearly see that all the cards are different.

- Close your eyes, then rub your index finger on your hair (or lack thereof), building static electricity.

- Still mixing the cards, with your eyes closed, name a random card and magically, one card magnetises to your index finger! The card rises fully from the deck and, despite all that shuffling, and being blindfolded, you have found the random card.

- The spectator asks if you have ever played *52-card pick-up*, and you pretend to laugh – because you are polite like that.

THE SECRET

So you want to know the secret? Fine, you've convinced me. I bow to your every wish.

As I said, all you need for this is a deck of cards. No special gimmicks – just a deck, and you're set to go. And now I'm going to break your heart – because the trick doesn't really rely on static electricity. I know – devastating. I can see your hopes and dreams crumbling around you.

First, I'll break down the method in its most basic form, then I'll teach you the moves in detail. Here's how the trick works.

- When no one is watching, before anyone knows that you're about to do the trick, secretly take a peek at the top card of the pack.

- When *shuffling* the cards, keep the top card in place, so it never moves. This way, you know which card is on top.

- When your eyes are closed or you're looking away, act as though you're naming a random card, then simply name the card that you *know* is on top.

- Then, you carry out a simple move, whereby the hidden pinky finger drags the card upwards, and seemingly out of the pack.

It's so simple once you see it in action. Just pay close attention to the following moves, which will help you perfect the trick.

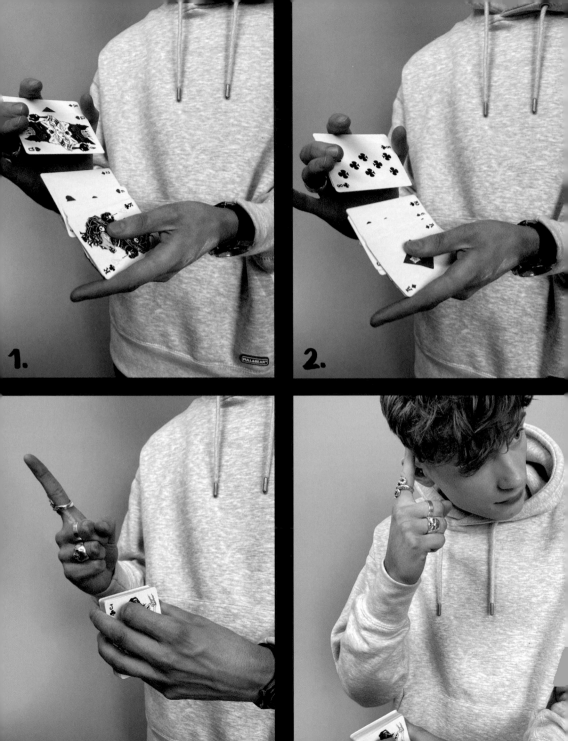

1.

2.

3.

4.

5.

6.

7.

8.

DETAIL: THE FALSE OVERHAND SHUFFLE

This move is worth learning, not only because it will enable you to accomplish this and many other tricks, but also because it allows you to cheat at cards fairly easily. Family poker nights just got a lot more interesting!

To perform the overhand shuffle:

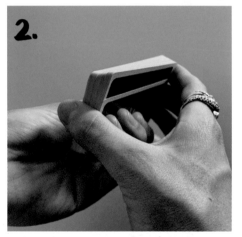

- Hold the pack in your non-dominant hand as shown, with your thumb on one end and your four fingers along the other.

- Now use your dominant hand to grip the cards with your four fingers on the back, and thumb on the faces.

- Add pressure, and begin to peel off cards, either one by one, or in small groups. Because of the pressure, the top card will stay in place, despite the others moving.

- Repeat as many times as you like.

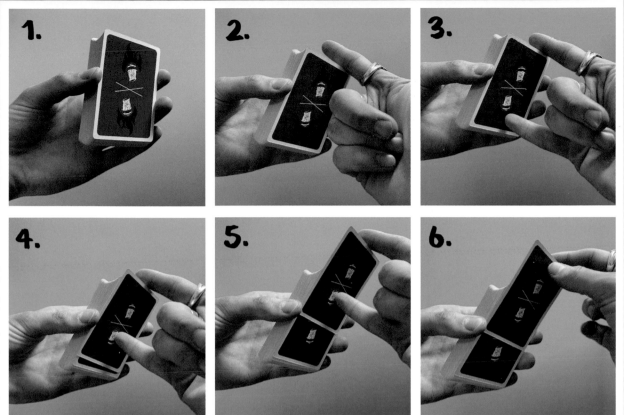

DETAIL: MAKING THE CARD RISE

To make the top card appear as though it is rising from the centre of the pack:

- Reposition the cards in your dominant hand with your four fingers along one edge and your thumb on the other. Turn your hand inwards so that the audience can see the faces of the cards.

- Now for the sneaky bit. Acting as though you are building a 'static charge', keep your index finger extended and place it along the top edge of the deck.

- Behind the cover of the deck, extend your pinky, and make contact with the top card. Move this hand in an upwards direction, while adding pressure to the top card. From the front angle, it will appear as though one card is magnetically rising from the deck!

- Act as though you are removing the card from the middle, show it around and enjoy your applause.

ALTERNATIVE METHOD

Let's say that you don't want to learn the false shuffle. That's fine, you can still do this trick.

Instead of memorising the top card, simply memorise the one that is fifth from the top. Then, instead of shuffling the cards, hold them in your hand as though you are about to do the rising-card move, but parallel to the floor, so the audience can see the top of the deck.

With your eyes closed, deal through the first four cards, asking the audience if they can see that all the cards are different. Place those cards aside, and then continue to do the rising card as before. The trick of displacing the top pile of cards will throw people off the scent of thinking you simply knew the top card.

And remember, the audience don't know that the card rises from the top of the deck. With some practice, and the correct positioning, it really will appear that the card rose from the centre. Therefore, knowing the top card wouldn't have helped you anyway.

So there you have it. An impromptu demonstration with a pack of playing cards. This trick has served me well over the years, and I hope you have as much fun performing it as I have.

PEN THROUGH BiLL

I still have the pen through bill illusion that I was gifted by my Papa all those years ago. It's a wonderful illusion that gets a powerful reaction from spectators, partly because of the reveal, but primarily due to the intolerable nature of destroying money. As they say, money doesn't grow on trees, so any trick that involves defacing cash guarantees attention from the spectator.

Trouble is, I don't want you to have to order a special pen or worry about preparing a special banknote. So I'm going to teach you a fantastic version of the pen through bill that you can do, impromptu, with very little practice.

THE TRICK

Here's what happens:

- You ask a spectator to borrow some money. Not realising that you're a magician, they refuse, assuming you are a beggar.

- You make a live lion appear to prove your worth.

- Amazed, the spectator hands over a £10 note. You then pull out a pen and hand it over to be examined. It is completely normal.

- You fold the note and place the tip of the pen on the inside of the fold. In one quick motion, stab the pen through the bill, so it visibly penetrates and can be seen going all the way through.

- Rip the pen through the bill to the side and hand the pen to the spectator. (Alarmed at this criminal offence, they may begin to hurl abuse at you.)

- A moment later, you rub the bill where it was torn and restore it back to its original state.

The spectator calms down, takes back the reincarnated £10 note and runs away from the hungry lion.

THE SECRET

Before I spill the beans on this one, I'm going to make a statement: I genuinely believe that this impromptu version of the pen through bill is better than the version that was bought for me! It's fast, visual and everything is examinable. Better still, it's incredibly easy to do. All you need is a banknote (not a plastic one) and a pen. Or, alternatively, you can use a receipt, a blank piece of paper and a pencil. Really, any thin, foldable object and something long and pointy will do.

The secret to this illusion lies in making a secret fold in the paper, allowing the pen to pass straight through, causing no damage.

Let's break it down:

- Either borrow or take out a banknote/ receipt/piece of paper. Show it to be completely normal.

- Take the paper and fold it as shown (see photo 2 overleaf), in an S-shaped manner.

- Remove a pen/pencil from your pocket and have it examined by the spectator. This acts as a diversion (a.k.a. misdirection) for the secret move you're about to perform!

- While the spectator is looking at the pen, use your thumb to create a secret fold on the inner portion of the paper, as shown (see photo 4 overleaf).

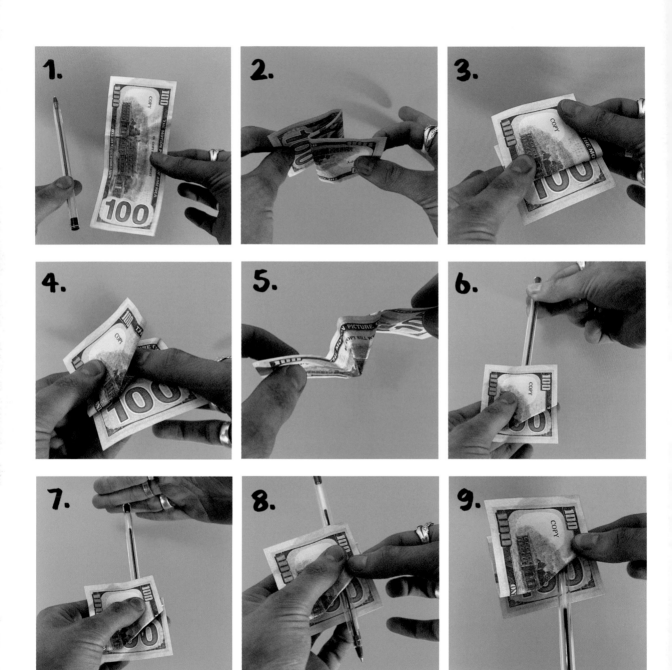

- Take the pen, and position it inside the bill, just above the secret fold. Whenever you're ready, push the pen through the fold swiftly. The sound of the pen sliding through the paper will create a sound similar to that of paper tearing.

- Pull the pen sideways out of the secret fold at a quick speed. That will create a sound similar to that of ripping the paper in two.

- Rub the *torn paper* and show that it has been magically restored.

This trick is a killer. The secret is simple, but honestly – this version fooled me badly when I first saw it.

A couple of things to watch out for: firstly, as mentioned above, the banknote should not be a plastic one. Although it might still work, the fold will be far too obvious and the spectator may be able to work out the method. Similarly, make sure the banknote isn't brand new; if it is, new creases will stick out like a sore thumb. It's worth being prepared and carrying your own note, just in case nobody has the right type – but give it to the spectator to confirm there is nothing suspicious about it. Otherwise, this trick is sure-fire and will absolutely floor audiences. And it's a great one to perform for people in a loud and busy setting because it doesn't require any dialogue to communicate the magic.

I'll always have a soft spot in my heart for this trick, as it takes me back so many years to when I was a kid, discovering my love of magic for the first time. I hope you love it as much as I do.

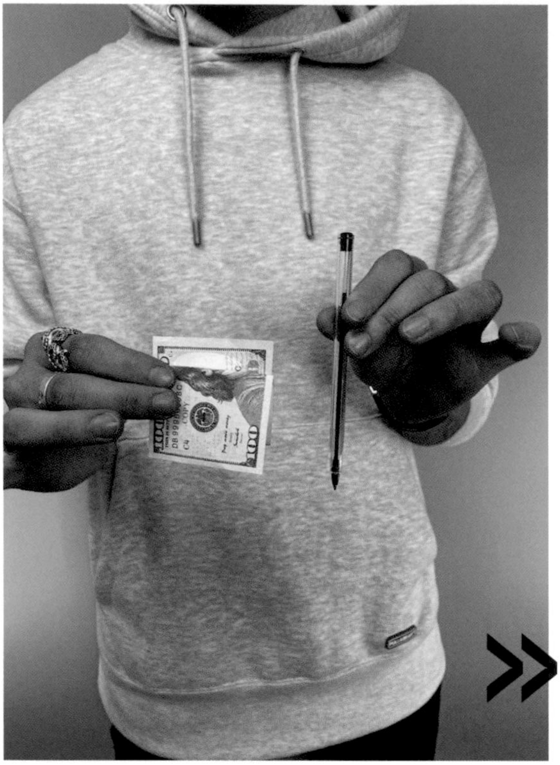

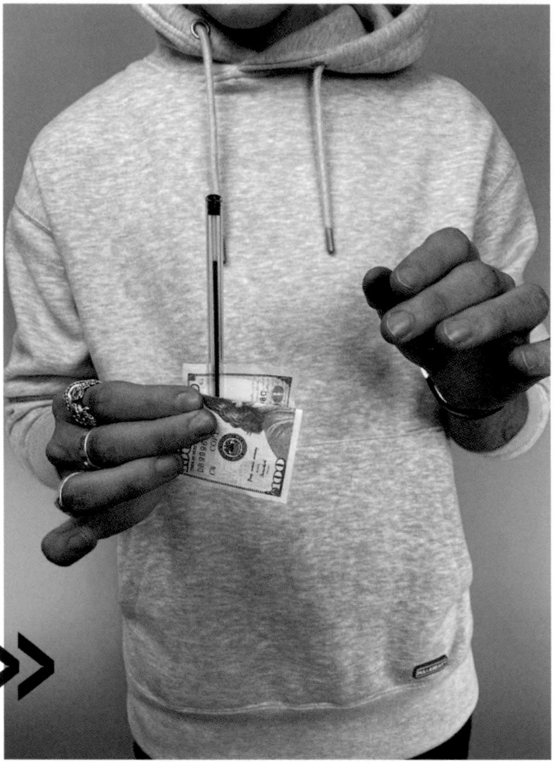

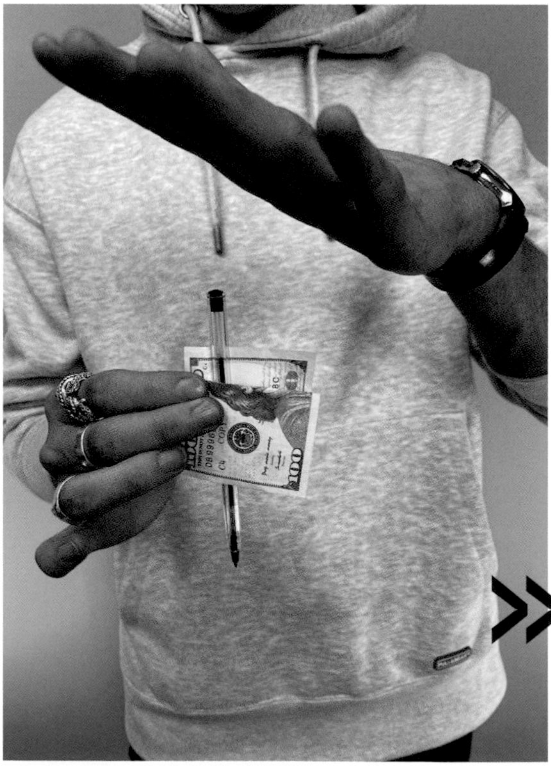

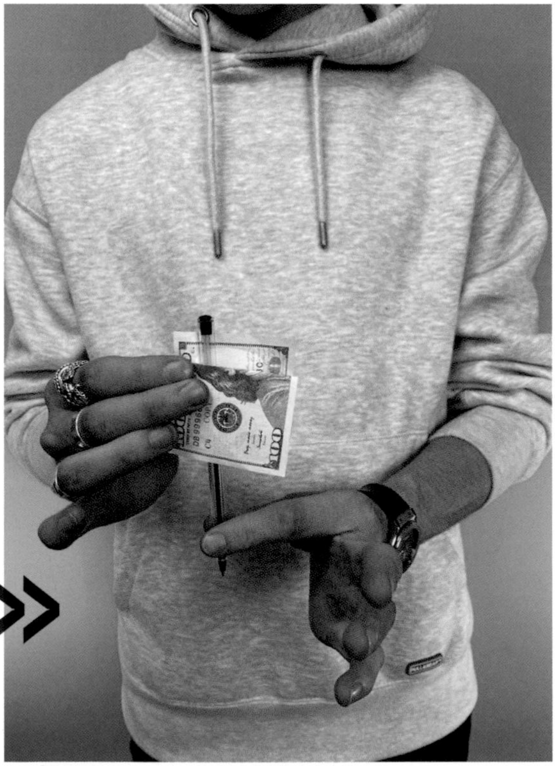

This trick is a killer. The secret is simple, but honestly – this version fooled me badly when I first saw it.

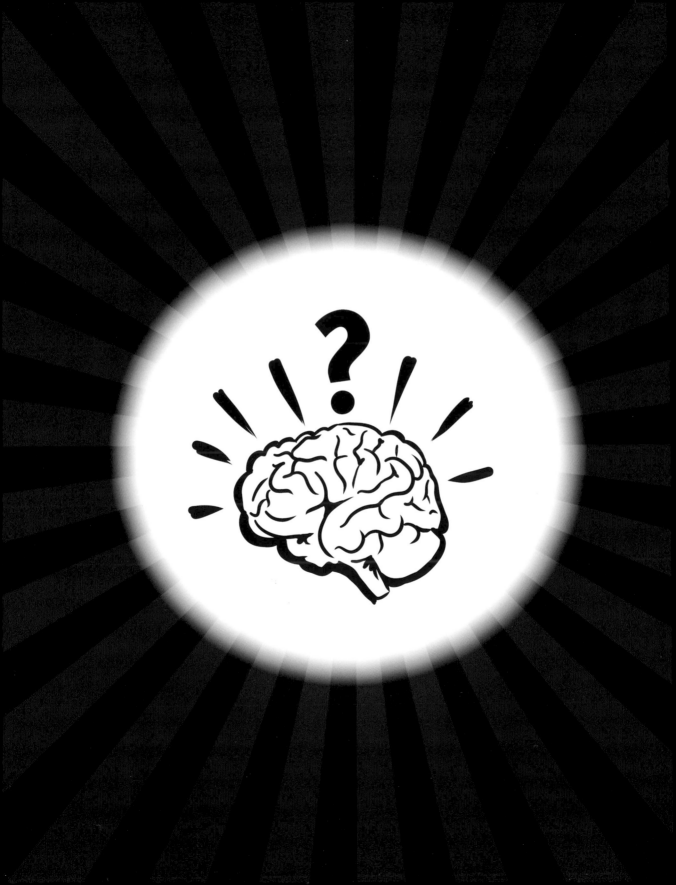

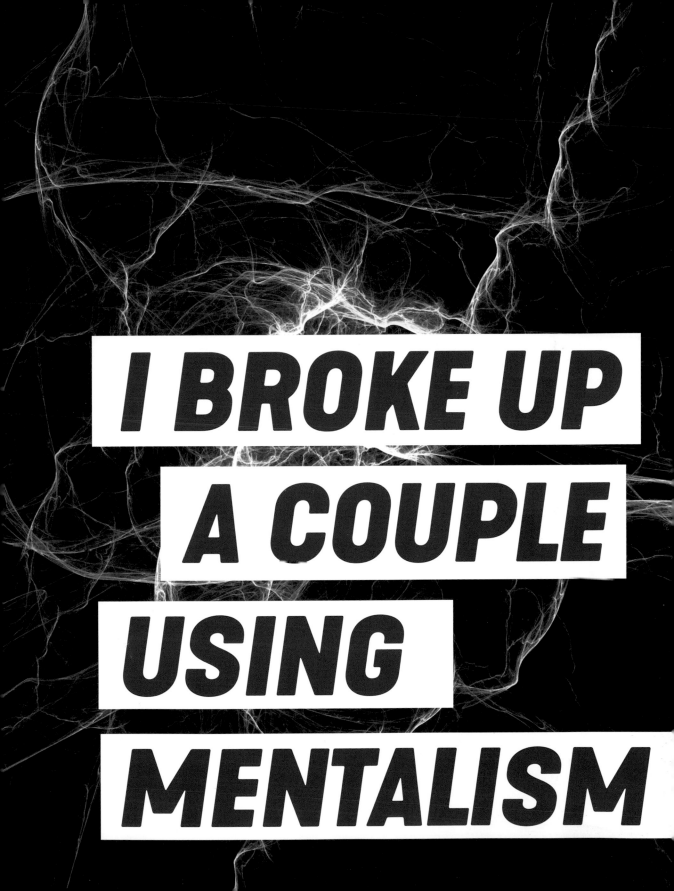

I've had the joy of performing at hundreds of events over the years, from kids' birthday parties in the beginning, to black-tie events, to massive festivals.

Actually, I should qualify that by saying I have really only performed at one kid's birthday party – and it was a disaster. I can still remember the infuriating child who climbed under the table and started searching through my close-up magic case, before revealing to the rest of the children that my tricks were not, in fact, *real magic*. Brat.

In all fairness, I was a kid myself at the time, so I couldn't exactly exert the required authority to enforce good behaviour from a room full of other children. I took my ten-pound Toys 'R' Us voucher as remittance and vowed never to perform at such an event again.

While I've kept that vow, I frequently get the opportunity to perform for kids, whether at weddings, family gatherings or sometimes on the street, when stopped by avid TikTok supporters. And believe it or not, I've often found it much more difficult to fool children with sleight of hand than adults. This is partly because kids are less prone to follow social cues and be misdirected by things that would distract an adult. But I think the main reason is that kids have fewer assumptions about the world – because an illusion is only possible if there is a previous assumption in the spectator's mind.

In a child's mind, *every* adult knows everything anyway. And by *reading their mind*, that's nothing more than what their parents can already do. It reminds me of when Nana used to tell me, '*Nanas know everything.*' I believed it for years. But one of the most startling realisations when entering adulthood, is that practically nobody really knows what they're doing – at all. We're all acting, some people are just better at it than others. Adulthood, in and of itself, is a massive illusion.

But why did I bring up performing for children in the first place? Well, having performed for thousands of people over the years, I've come to terms with the fact that adults frequently act like children, too. Especially when they are handed a microphone and put in the spotlight. In fact, a survey once revealed the startling fact that most people fear public speaking, more than death. That's not a joke – that's a real study. Look it up – complete madness!

> It's often not until somebody steps in front of a large group of people that they realise how difficult it is to not be a total weirdo. Trust me, I've learned the hard way . . . my first full cabaret show was borderline unwatchable.

So most people go to pieces when on stage, and those who don't either have such a burning desire to be a performer that they are willing to go through the tortuous humiliation of being laughed at or, in very rare cases, they have a natural talent. (I went through the tortuous humiliation!) Therefore, as you can imagine, as a performer who constantly brings people on stage and one whose show is entirely audience interactive, I've witnessed my fair share of cringeworthy moments. Allow me to share one with you.

Let me take you on a journey to one of my favourite events of all time: Midweek Magic. At the time of writing, I live in the centre of Belfast (come and find me, stalkers). And out of all the events I've ever performed at, the one that always brought me the most joy was Midweek Magic.

Every second Wednesday of every month, since I was twelve years old (and until the arrival of Covid-19), this wonderful little show has taken place in the middle of the wonderful city. Four magicians, four hours – and all for a £4 ticket.

This show is *serious* fun. The perfect opportunity to improve, to test new material and hang out with other magicians. I have my fingers well and truly crossed for the return of Midweek Magic once the world is back to its safer norm.

Essentially, the four magicians would perform, table to table, doing close-up magic for about forty guests. Those magicians would also have the chance to perform on the stage. Such a wonderful idea.

I dread to think of the number of awful routines I've brought to that stage over the years, but it gave me the perfect platform to be bad, with a forgiving, receptive audience. If you ever get the chance to go, you should. And you'll probably find me there.

But no event is perfect, and of course, with its low ticket price, we often got some strange characters in through the door. This story is about one in particular.

I must have been about seventeen years old and smack bang in the middle of my Colin-Cloud-meets-Derren-Brown phase. It was around the time that I was starting to get pretty decent at stage performance, and I was beginning to

try out more and more daring routines. One of my favourites was – and still is – the embarrassing memory routine.

Reading minds at 'Midweek Magic'.

My time to perform at Midweek Magic had arrived, and up I went to the stage, introduced by the wonderful magician Caolan McBride. As a side note, Caolan was the first magician I ever met in Northern Ireland. (Caolan, if you're reading this, I probably wouldn't be doing magic without your help. You gave me a helping hand and introductions I never would have made myself. Thank you for that.)

I opened by performing the human blockhead, where I hammer a very real nail into my nose. Not one for the weak hearted, but one that certainly gets the crowd interested. I had one full set of GCSEs and was halfway through my A-Levels, and there I was, hammering a nail into my face. What an intelligent life decision.

Once I had pulled out the nail, taken my applause and cleaned up the inevitable nose bleed, I then moved on to the embarrassing memory routine. It starts with me inviting three random audience members to join me on the stage. Typically,

IT WAS A CONFESSION. A CONFESSION OF BEING CAUGHT DOING SOMETHING . . . UNSAVOURY. IN A VERY PUBLIC PLACE. WHATEVER IT IS YOU'RE GUESSING AT RIGHT NOW, I CAN PROMISE YOU, THE REALITY WAS WORSE. AN ABSOLUTELY MORTIFYING, POSSIBLY EVEN CRIMINAL CONFESSION THAT NO ONE IN THEIR RIGHT MIND WOULD OPENLY ADMIT TO A ROOM FULL OF STRANGERS!

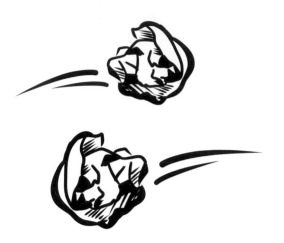

these are spectators chosen by throwing a crumpled-up paper ball around the room and having those who happen to be lucky enough to catch it waltz up to the stage.

However, on this evening, the paper ball found itself in the sweaty palms of a rather uncouth gentleman. I remember him well – quite a tall, looming figure, but with a pudgy face. When performing close-up magic for him and his partner earlier in the evening, I remember being shocked at his bad manners and severe halitosis.

I knew before even getting started that this man would be a substandard choice for the demonstration. But asking a spectator to refrain from appearing on stage is not only rude, it also makes the selection process less random. As such, the man who had apparently failed to make use of his toothbrush over the last two days left his seat and joined me up on the stage.

Two more participants were selected at random, and they too made their way to the front of the room. So: three spectators, one magician. And for once, the magician wasn't the strangest person on the stage. A rare occurrence.

'I'd like each of you to think of an embarrassing memory,' I explained to the volunteers, 'and once you've thought of something, scribble it down on this piece of paper, but don't let anybody see it. Keep it a secret, but make sure it's something you'd be happy to share later with the room.' That last sentence is key.

The participants did as requested, sneakily jotting down some distant, ignominious echo of the past. It's worth pointing out that typically, when I'm performing this routine, the lion's share of people choose to focus on something marginally funny, but rarely something truly embarrassing. Something like 'I fell off my bike' or, 'I forgot my times tables in front of my classmates'. All harmless fun. Nothing incriminating.

Not so, in this rare case.

My job, as the enigmatic mentalist, is to divine what has been thought of. Naturally, I do so without asking to read the paper on which the participants have scribbled down their confession. (That would merely be reading, not mind reading.)

I won't get into the method behind this trick, as it's one that I still perform today, and I'd quite like to amaze you with it one day in person. Suffice it to say, however, I have, one way or another, developed the means to deduce the memories that lie within the skull of a human being standing on stage. Mind reading. Or so it appears.

The goal of the trick is for me to correctly proclaim to the crowd which memory each person has thought of. It's the sort of trick that has brought the house down on more than one occasion. It's a comical joy to perform.

I very quickly realised, however, that this slightly strange gentleman had thought of something that

. . . well, something I wouldn't feel comfortable writing in my debut book!

It was a confession. A confession of being caught doing something . . . unsavoury. In a very public place. Whatever it is you're guessing at right now, I can promise you, the reality was worse. An absolutely mortifying, possibly even criminal confession that no one in their right mind would openly admit to a room full of strangers!

Having no pressing desire to reveal this information, I made the snap decision to focus on the other two participants first. I correctly revealed their memories – to the amazement of the room – and they returned to their seats. Which left me with the oddball.

I was now facing a dilemma. On the one hand, I could simply skip over the final memory, send him to his seat and wrap up the show. But in that case, everyone, including the man himself, would assume that I had simply got the trick wrong. And the man would almost certainly heckle – something I like to avoid at all costs. The only other option was to reveal to the crowd the horrible memory the man had thought of.

I decided to go with the latter.

At the very least, I thought, I'll get a good laugh out of the situation. And let's face it – I had stipulated that the memory must be something that they'd be willing to share with the room. He had signed up for his own downfall. So I went in for the kill.

'Yes or no: are you thinking of the time you _____?'

'Yes!' exclaimed the man, in a state of total excitement.

I couldn't believe it. There was absolutely no shame. If anything, he seemed proud. Giddy, maybe, but certainly not shameful.

Thankfully, feeling my awkwardness, the audience greeted me with tumultuous applause and roaring laughter. I suppose I had, after all, got the trick right. So I gestured in the direction of the gentleman's seat, cueing his leave.

Which is when I noticed that his partner was nowhere to be seen. She was gone. Probably just using the bathroom, I thought. But not so. The poor lady never came back. The strange man sat alone, sipping his ale, apparently oblivious to the fact that every person in the room considered him a total nut case. Ignorance is bliss.

After the show, I spoke to my friend who was running the event. It turned out that the incompatible pair were, in fact, on a first date, and having witnessed him on stage, the woman had clearly seen more than enough to decide that this gentleman was not to be her life partner. She left the moment I announced the hideous memory.

So that's £4 well spent, I think. And if you ever find yourself at one of my shows – or any mentalism show, for that matter – mind your thoughts. You never know who might be reading them.

PREDICT THE FUTURE

Reading this story, you may be wondering, how can someone read minds? It's a good question. Is it psychology? Is it years of disciplined practice of the deductive arts? Or is it mere trickery?

I couldn't possibly say.

However, I would love to share with you a fun little trick you can use to blow the minds of others. I'm going to teach you how to predict the future. A big claim, I know, but it's impromptu, works any time and will make you look like a mathematical genius.

THE TRICK

Here's what happens:

- You grab a piece of paper or a napkin – whatever's to hand – and scribble something down, unseen by your volunteer. They will wonder what it is – an evil curse, an ancient spell . . . Only time will tell.

- You then ask your volunteer to think of a three-digit number and type it into the calculator on their phone. But tell them, to make it more random and more challenging for you, to make sure that all the digits are different. So nothing obvious, like 333, 444, etc.

- Tell the spectator to reverse that number in their head. So if they thought of 123, they would now be thinking of 321. Make sense?

- Tell them that to make this incredibly random they should subtract whichever their smaller number from their bigger number and then hit equals.

- To jumble things up one final time, tell the spectator to take the number on their screen and reverse it, so that they have an entirely new number, then to add that new number to the one already on their screen. Then hit equals again without letting you see *anything*.

- So you have a final number. You say to the spectator, 'Can we both agree that had you thought of a number even one digit different at the beginning, you would now have a totally different answer?'

- You then turn over the piece of paper you wrote on at the start of the trick, and – lo and behold – you predicted your volunteer's final number, right down to the last digit. They are amazed and fully convinced of the power of prediction.

THE SECRET

The good news for you is that explaining the mathematics behind what makes this trick work is not only beyond me, but not necessary either. All you need to know is that if you trust me and follow these instructions perfectly, this trick will work every single time.

No matter what number the spectator starts off with, the total will always be **1089**. How? Haven't got a clue. But that's not important. What it means, however, is that before you begin the trick, all you have to do is 'predict' the outcome: write down 1089. Write it on a piece of paper, on a coffee cup, get an aeroplane to scroll it across the sky, for all I care, but just make sure you remember 1089.

If you doubt the maths, try it for yourself now. Here's an example:

123 reversed is 321.

$$321 - 123 = 198$$

198 reversed is 891.

$$981 + 189 = 1089$$

You might be anxious to perform this, in case the spectator backtracks and figures out that the outcome is always the same. But I've found that as long as you don't repeat the trick, people are not only amazed, but also forget the steps they took in order to get the total, so it helps to distract them with jokes, good cheer and plenty of charm. Of course, this trick could easily come across as a lame mathematical puzzle if you don't present it correctly. Draw their attention to your prediction and their free choice, rather than the equation itself, making sure to keep it all fun and light-hearted.

Simply trust the process and blow some minds.

PS I've yet to figure out how to predict lottery numbers, but when I do, I assure you, you'll never know.

TELEKINESIS GONE WRONG

Throughout my life, one thing I've consistently been called is obsessed.

Friends, family and I guess anyone who has met me will tell you that I have a ferocious focus, probably to a fault. I have a terrible tendency to zone out of conversations completely and get locked into a thought.

This has been both a good and a bad thing. On one hand, being obsessive led me to a Minecraft addiction for three years solid. (Big shout-out to CJ for the endless pixelated fun.) On the other hand, it's also allowed me to work eighteen-hour days for weeks in a row in order to accomplish a particular goal. For example, being obsessed with hitting a target of 2 million social media followers, I streamed live on the internet for twenty-four hours straight. I then slept for three hours and got right back to it. Ridiculous. Unhealthy. But obsessive.

Although being so immersed in a particular thing definitely has its downfalls, it has allowed me to do a lot of the things I've wanted to do at a fairly young age. From the second I saw Derren Brown perform on stage, I was obsessed. It wasn't that I wanted to do the same thing; I *needed* to do the same thing. And for years, it's all I cared about. It became my biggest obsession, my north star, my dream.

Although I managed to get through school with good grades (primarily down to some memory techniques I picked up via mentalism books), the best part of my teenage years was spent dreaming up ideas for magic shows and rehearsing in my bedroom. I'd use my bedroom as a makeshift stage, spending hours and hours mapping everything out, setting up theatre shows next to my desk and running them through with imaginary volunteers. For some reason, I always

chose to call the volunteers Karen. Honestly, I don't know why.

It wasn't all for nothing though. At the age of seventeen, I sold tickets to my first live mentalism show. And I can't even begin to tell you how rewarding that was! I'm sure it was terrible, of course, but you've got to start somewhere.

Looking back, the times where I haven't been obsessed, or driven, have been the worst of my life. I need something to pursue, to fill every second of my day, or I go crazy. That's just the kind of person I am.

Of course, it can be frustrating for those close to me – so a massive thank you to everyone who deals with my magical nonsense. I'm not a diva, but I do take what I do seriously. And I think you should, too.

At any rate, I have been obsessed with performing on a stage all my life. And it's still my dream. The reason I've spent the last couple of years building a presence online is that one day, I'd love all those people to come and see me in a live show.

But of course, on the road towards a dream, we all make mistakes, and I've made plenty. You've already read about some of them, and in most cases, any mistakes on stage have been merely moments of mental pain. Sheer embarrassment. However, I'd like to take you back to a time where the mistake I made caused more than just psychological humiliation – the time I seriously injured myself while on stage.

It was Christmas time, maybe two or three days before Santa was due to arrive. I remember because the snow was absurd. And it was my third public theatre show. One hundred and fifty seats sold out. Proud, but also nervous. The show was called *Impossible Peculiarities*, *and Other Significant Mysteries*.' (Talk about pretentious! My latest show was called, *Joel M, Magician*. Much more understated.)

When I was writing the show with my wonderful friend Shane, we thought it would be a fun idea to create a trick that used a piano. We didn't consider the fact that we'd need to bring a piano to the venue of course.

Obsessed, but not organised.

Infuriatingly, although there was a grand piano already at the theatre, whoever designed the place had clearly decided it would be a good idea to make the doors so small that it was impossible to actually get the instrument into the auditorium. So my very kind friends and family provided the extra muscle needed to load my own smaller piano into the back of a van and we drove it to the theatre ourselves. It was freezing cold, and we slipped and fell countless times on the icy paths.

But it was worth it. The piano trick was the best part of the show, and still, to this day, the best trick I've worked on. Thanks, Shane, for your creative genius.

However . . . you win some, you lose some. A magic show on a chilly Christmas evening. Two hours of mystery and fun. What could possibly go wrong?

Me off stage during my one-man show 'Phobia'.

The first half of the show was great: the tricks worked, the audience were engaged and everything was going to plan. Nailed the piano trick. No complaints. That was until the interval. You see, the second half of the show was focused entirely around the concept of *telekinesis*.

Telekinesis is an alleged psychic ability allowing a person to influence a physical system without physical interaction. Let me be clear here: I am not and do not claim to be psychic. But I do have a lot of fun creating the illusion of being so. Think Eleven from *Stranger Things*.

With a combination of sleight of hand, misdirection and clever props, a magician can create the impression that they are, in fact, psychic. I use it purely for entertainment, of course, and I always tell the audience that what I'm doing is mere trickery.

In any case, the show was based around that concept, and I suggested to the audience that during the interval they might want to leave any item they'd like me to attempt a demonstration with in a designated box at the front of the stage. By the time I walked back on stage for the second half of the show, the box was overflowing with all sorts of items: old keys, receipts, all the way to mobile phones. People had done exactly what I asked for. Time to play.

I began by taking a pair of sunglasses and making them move without touching them. Not bad! Moving on, I caused the stem of a wine glass to bend, leaving an astounded woman with a very cool souvenir. Even better.

A couple of demonstrations on, I reached into the box and my fingers landed upon a light bulb. Fantastic! I had just the right trick – one I hoped would blow the audience away.

Holding the light bulb in my hand, I asked for all the lights inside the theatre to be turned off. It was pitch black.

And then . . . a spark of light!

With the help of a secret technique, which, sadly, I can't teach you (or else the magic police will come and arrest me), the light bulb flickered and then shone brightly in my hand. Gasps, of course!

The trick was cool, but I wanted to take it to another level.

My *bright* idea was to make the light bulb explode, using 'telekinesis', of course. I had a method in mind to make it work, but had never actually attempted it on stage before. First time for everything . . .

I asked Ethan, my stagehand at the time, to run and get me a clear ziplock bag from the café kitchen. He went off, returning a few moments later, bag in hand.

I placed the light bulb inside the bag and, addressing a lady in the front row, said: 'Madame, if you would be so kind, could you seal this bag shut and hold it with your fingertips? Perfect. Now, watch closely.'

I focused all my attention on the bulb and unleashed my inner Uri Geller.

The crowd was silent, unsure as to what was going to happen next. Then . . .

Crack.

Well, when I say that the result was underwhelming, I mean it. I had been aiming to make the light bulb shatter into a thousand pieces, but it was not to be. One measly little crack in the bulb was all that resulted from my immense telekinetic efforts. I guess Luke Skywalker makes it look too easy.

Regardless, the crack seemed to be enough to marginally impress the crowd, and a light scatter of applause met my ears. And that was when I had a *fantastic* idea.

You see, the stage was relatively dark, and people's eyesight is only so good. I figured that if I were to simply squeeze the bulb, now that it was cracked, it would shatter. And if I could somehow cover this move with some misdirection, I might be able to convince the audience that it was, in fact, a miracle.

I gave it my best shot. Upon taking the ziplock bag back, I lightly squeezed the bulb, covering the obvious motion with a grandiose snap of my fingers. To my relief, it shattered. And seemingly, the move had gone over the heads of the majority of the audience, for the applause I had initially sought finally arrived. Nothing thunderous, but probably more than I deserved.

And so I was happy. Time to move on to the next trick. The banknote divination.

'Everyone, pull out your wallets,' I instructed, slightly more aggressively than intended, but it certainly got my point across. Everyone in the room pulled out their wallets or purses.

'If you have one, remove a banknote from your wallet and fold it up, so that nobody can see the serial number. Once you've done that, hold the note in your fist, above your head.'

About fifty people clenched their cash in their fists, high up in the air. Time to bring out the trusty paper ball, to select a random audience member. I threw it out into the crowd, gently plonking a poor soul on the head. I should have realised that having one hand out of action, made catching slightly more difficult! Still, I had my volunteer: a short, little man, who had followed my instructions perfectly. He stood up, continuing to hold the note tightly in his hand.

'Sir, is there any way that I could possibly know what type of banknote you're holding?'

'Not unless you've got X-ray vision!' he replied.

Damn it, he had figured out the method . . . Kidding, of course. I'm no Henry Cavill.

'I wish! Listen, I'm going to close my eyes. And when I do, I'd like you to place that note inside my hand. I won't look. Watch me carefully to make sure I don't cheat!'

He did as directed.

At this point, it was my job to somehow divine the serial number on the banknote. How? Well, that would be telling. But what I can say is that for the trick to work, I needed to *feel* the banknote, so I could at least figure out what kind I was working with. So I started to move my fingers around, trying to gauge the size.

What on earth . . . ?

The note felt strange. I could tell that it was one of those new plastic ones. But it was as though the man had covered it with Vaseline. It felt disgusting, slimy. But why?

I started to sweat. This can't be good, I thought.

A slight throbbing feeling started in my hand. The throbbing turned into a shake. And then it hit me. The note wasn't covered in Vaseline. It was covered in blood. My blood! And considering the fact that I could clearly tell the note was a twenty, the gentleman wasn't going to be too pleased.

You're probably putting two and two together right now. Yes – you guessed it: the light bulb.

I had been so focused on making the trick work that I hadn't even felt the glass slip through the ziplock bag, and slice open my finger. I was totally oblivious. I told you that I tend to zone out – remember?

So I'm standing in the aisle, all eyes on me, holding a £20 note in my hand, which is dripping in blood. My next move wasn't particularly smart, or safe, but I decided to go for it.

'I believe the serial number is . . .' And I announced the series of random digits I had somehow deduced. I knew I was correct. The trouble was, I had to have the numbers confirmed.

So I handed the note back to the poor gentleman.

It was scarlet. Drenched. So much so that the man didn't want to take it back. And rightly so!

The audience were confused, but I eventually managed to wipe off the gore and have my prediction confirmed as correct. At least the trick had worked. And I muttered a swift promise to the man that I'd replace his note with one less disgusting after the show.

By now, my hand was shaking violently, and as I walked back to the stage, I realised how badly I'd cut it. Very.

Nevertheless, I continued with the final trick of the evening. The big finale.

Fuelled with adrenaline, the pain subsiding, I got back into the zone.

'Please, could somebody genuinely get me a bandage and some water,' I asked. 'I've cut my finger!'

But no such help arrived. And, of course, I should have known why.

Everyone thought it was part of the show. And let's face it, all evening I'd been spinning a web of pure lies. Why should anyone have taken anything I said seriously?

I made direct eye contact with my cameraman and finally got the message across. A few moments later, he arrived with a massive handful of toilet paper and a glass of water. That was good enough.

Having soaked my hand in the water, unintentionally performing an impromptu water-into-wine illusion, I wrapped up my finger in toilet roll and ended the show.

I'd given it my all – every ounce of showmanship and energy I could muster. The lights went down, and I made my way backstage.

Success. (If you excuse the blood everywhere.)

As it turns out, there was shattered glass inside my finger, and for the next two weeks, I couldn't move it at all – which was ultra-fun when performing close-up magic the next day at a corporate party.

I did learn one thing, though.

When I went out to the gallery to meet my wonderful audience, get photos and chat among them, I found out that despite the obvious wound, the blood and everything else that had happened, most people still thought that the whole thing was part of the trick. That somehow, the wound was a distraction to help me pull off the final trick! They gave me far too much credit. I'm just clumsy.

I usually wrap up these stories with some sort of life lesson. But truthfully, the only lesson to be learned here is: don't be a moron like me and squeeze a light bulb.

But I feel like you probably already knew that.

PS I have since dropped the light-bulb illusion from my show.

TRICK TOK THREE:
PLAYING THE ONLINE GAME

You may be thinking that you're ready to get started, armed will all the new information we've looked at. But although you certainly have an advantage now, we haven't even touched on the most important stuff.

CLARITY OVER EVERYTHING

Whether you're creating video, photo or audio content, you need to follow one rule.

Never. Be. Confusing.

I know. That sounds bizarre coming from a magician whose entire career is built around confusing people. But hear me out.

The biggest mistake I see people making (and one I have made, and still do from time to time) is being confusing.

Lack of clarity will kill your social media growth.

A confused viewer won't stick with you. So things need to be clear. Which means a whole bunch of different things – from clear lighting to clear messaging. Is your video quality unclear? People will swipe. Is your niche unclear? People won't follow. Is your video topic all over the show? People will lose interest.

If, at any point, you think a viewer might be confused as to what they should be paying attention to, you need to change that. I'd go as far as to literally tell the viewer what they should be paying attention to. Spoon-feed them the content, spelling out exactly what you're doing. And keep it simple.

If you're a dance teacher, make it clear what you're teaching. Don't take the conversation off to Pluto; you need to stay focused, and present your piece of content as a clear, concise package.

I was awful at this for years. I could take a really nice, strong video idea and complicate it until it was an utterly convoluted mess. So take the classic advice, and KISS: Keep. It. Simple. Stupid. (I don't actually think you're stupid!) Anyone can make a messy, complicated video. It takes effort to simplify it and achieve clarity.

DON'T CARE WHAT PEOPLE THINK

Ok, I'm about to give you some cold, hard truth.

Not everyone is going to like you.

In fact, a lot of people *aren't* going to like you! And the sooner you can accept that, the better.

I follow a simple rule: for every one person who loves me, there's probably going to be one who doesn't like me. And that's ok.

Listen, the worst thing you can ever do is try to please everyone, all of the time. You'll die trying. It's better to recognise that you're going to have people who aren't fans, and focus your attention on those who are!

I get asked about haters all the time. Mostly: 'Do you get haters?' Or, 'Do hate comments get to you?'

Firstly, of course I get haters. Everyone does. It's just on a different level when you promote online. And secondly, yes, sometimes their comments do get to me, but not nearly as much as they used to, or as much as they affect most other people. That's the truth.

And let me tell you, dealing with haters in a healthy way does not come easy. I'm a natural-born people pleaser. Ask any one of my friends or family, and they'll tell you that growing up, I'd bend over backwards to avoid conflict.

So how do I deal with it? And, more importantly, how can you?

But first, it's worth saying this: before you jump into the world of social media, please make sure that you're mentally robust enough to handle any negative fallout.

I mean that. I've seen people torn apart by comments online. It's a game that just isn't for everyone – and although I always suggest that people follow their dreams, make sure first that you're ready to get backlash from people.

Ok, so how do we deal with haters? I certainly don't have all the answers, but the advice I'm about to give you has helped me immensely over the last few years.

Let me start with something one of my mentors told me: lions don't lose sleep over the opinions of sheep.

It's blunt, but it's true. You simply cannot allow yourself to be dragged down by the naysayers. And trust me, they'll try. Even people you've known for years will stop supporting you, especially if things start to take off. So I'd rather you be ready for it to happen than surprised and upset when it does.

Anyone, and I mean *anyone* who tries to drag you down – whether it's a hate comment on a social media post or a backhanded comment at a family dinner – is acting like a sheep. Let them follow the crowd and deal with their own problems. All you have to do is focus on what you want and not allow anyone to take up your mental headspace with negativity. As I say, lions don't lose sleep over the opinions of sheep.

Think about it this way. If someone has the time to take a moment out of their day, just to try and kick you down, they're clearly not the type of person that's doing anything of much importance themselves.

It's extremely rare that you'll get hate from someone who is already doing what they love, and successful at it. Most hate comments come from anonymous people on the web, who, should you ever have the chance to meet them in real life, wouldn't say a word.

Most hate comes from a place of jealousy. The only reason they feel the need to bring you down is so that they can feel above you . . . and maybe even feel a little better about themselves for a minute. Pity them.

I'm very proud to say, that I've never, ever left a hate comment. But if you have, or still do . . . stop. Not for me, but for you. All you're doing is hurting yourself in the process.

The sooner you realise that the reason someone has left hate is almost always because it has touched upon some insecurity of their own, the easier it is to brush them off. Sure, now and again I still get annoyed by comments about silly things, but the second I do, I bounce it out of my head.

I refuse to let the opinion of another person (especially one who
I will likely never meet) impact the pursuit of my goals. Ever.
You shouldn't either.

Quick note. I do not recommend that you respond to haters or trolls.
You can if you like, but I find it to be a waste of time. It's unlikely that
you'll change their minds, and even if you do, so what? They were
clearly not all that invested in the argument in the first place.
It's a waste of your time and mental energy.

Oh, and make no mistake – it is 100 per cent ok for you to delete hate
comments or block people who are being in any way cruel. Personally,
I don't even bother, as they don't affect me all that much. But out of
sight, out of mind – so don't let an irritating message take up a even
moment of your day.

Let me give you an example about a time I received a pretty nasty
hate comment.

I posted a video I was incredibly proud of. It went viral. Really viral.
Over 100 million views! The most I had ever received on a piece of
content online. Naturally, I was ecstatic.

However, after a long day of filming, when I wasn't in the best
headspace to read comments, I made the mistake of looking –
and trust me, if you go looking for something bad, you'll find it.

I saw a comment that made fun of the size of my forehead – something
that's been an insecurity of mine for years – and for a brief moment,
it really upset me. So much so that I almost took the video down.
I figured that if one person commented on it, lots of people must
have been thinking it, too.

Then I realised. Who cares?

Firstly, my forehead is fine. Sure, I could maybe do with an extra inch
of hairline, but whatever – the fringe covers it. (That's what I usually tell
myself, anyway.)

But secondly, and more significantly, I had just let the opinion of one
anonymous person completely blind me to the fact that millions of

others had enjoyed the video and even shared it. That one hate comment had stood out and held more importance in my mind than all the other comments combined. Until, that is, I decided not to let it.

That person knew nothing about my goals, my thoughts or anything else about me, for that matter. Let's face it, even our closest family and friends don't know everything about us – so why should we take the opinion of somebody who knows absolutely nothing about us seriously.

As far as I'm aware, we get one shot at this thing. This isn't a trial run. So don't let somebody else steal your dream.

I'm telling you this for two reasons. Firstly, to show you that sometimes even I get frustrated with haters, but the key is to put things into perspective, realise that it says more about them than it does about you and move on. And secondly, I told you in the hope that if you ever do consider leaving a negative comment, you'll think again. Just one hate comment could absolutely ruin somebody. So please think before you type. Your words hold great power. Use them for good.

And now, a few final practical points.

Firstly, if you're serious about social media, learn to love the haters. Because they pay. Literally. I know for a fact that my haters rewatch and share my videos even more than my fans. And guess what: that's nothing but a good thing for the bank account. So when you see a hate comment, think £. That alone will help you care less about what people say about you. So long as they're saying something, it's all good.

Also, a lot of the hate comments I receive aren't meant to be taken seriously. In fact, most of the time, when I used to engage with them, I'd get a reply saying that they just wanted to get my attention. So take every hater with a pinch of salt. Sometimes they just want recognition and can't think of a positive way to get it, so they resort to nonsensical, hateful trolling.

As American author David Foster Wallace once said: 'You'd worry less about what people think of you, when you realise how seldom they do.'

Growing up, I always wanted to be on TV. Most likely because that's where I'd seen all of my idols thrive. I loved shows like *Trick of the Mind*, *Mindfreak*, *Fool Us*, to name just a few.

The idea of performing on TV was very cool to me; so much so that I passed on many great opportunities for exposure over the years. Let's face it, the internet has been around for a long time now, but it took me years and years before I actually started taking it seriously, and I didn't even consider the possibility that social media could help me get a TV show. In fact, I only started really taking it seriously by accident. So here is the story of how my magic went viral – not through brains, but by pure luck.

I was nineteen and had just left school. Out into the real world, ready to try and make my mark. In truth, I didn't really know what making my mark meant. All I knew was that I wanted to be a magician – I loved magic, and that was enough for now.

I spent most of my time planning, planning and planning some more. I never really did anything all that useful. I never moved the needle. You see, I had all these *fantastic ideas*, but it would take me months, sometimes years to act on them. And this was amplified tenfold when it came to posting on social media.

Over the course of a year, from age nineteen to twenty, I posted *three* videos online. Three. I justified this by telling myself that 'quality over quantity' was the goal. Trouble was, the lack of practice – i.e. quantity – meant that I never got to produce anything of quality.

At nineteen, I had 300 subscribers on YouTube. Goodness knows who was watching those videos – they were totally abysmal. And I'm not being

self-deprecating for no reason. Honestly. (You can go back and find them if you fancy a good laugh!) But it all changed when I met Shane and Kymann. Two of my best friends in the world, they are creative, funny, kind and hard-working fellas, who, for some reason, took a liking to me. I certainly took a liking to them.

Having created their own fair share of social media content, Shane and Kymann convinced me that I should be doing the same. Logically, I knew this, of course, but sometimes it just takes someone other than yourself for you to get up and do something.

The three of us got together in Belfast with the intention of shooting a street magic YouTube video. I had it all planned out in my head, and with loads of tricks in mind to entertain random passersby, we hit the streets.

With iPhone cameras at the ready, we began to shoot. I think we got ten seconds of footage before the heavens opened and rain began to pour down to such an extent that we were forced to run into the nearest form of shelter available.

That shelter was Tesco.

After thirty minutes of standing around the meal-deal section, waiting for the rain to stop, we came to terms with the fact that Northern Ireland was clearly unforgiving when it came to rain, and that we weren't going to be filming outside any time soon.

We decided instead to wander around the supermarket. Unable to help myself, I started messing around with some of the items on the shelves, performing impromptu magic. Never a dull moment.

I picked up a lemon, threw it into the air and, with a magic wave, it multiplied into two.

'That's it!' said Shane.

'That's what?' I asked.

'That's the video . . . you doing magic in a supermarket,' he replied.

I wasn't convinced. Why would anyone in their right mind want to watch that? It would be ridiculous. After all, it hadn't been done online before – and with good reason.

'He's right,' said Kymann. 'I think it'd get thousands of views.'

Still unconvinced, but outnumbered, I decided to give it a try.

As you can imagine, we got some very, very unusual looks, as cereal boxes transformed, chocolates disappeared and I even put a coin through a sealed bottle of water. (As the comments section still likes to remind me, that could have been a serious choking hazard. Ooops.)

The hardest part of the entire experience was filming in the biscuit aisle. It took us forty minutes to film a ten-second magic trick without someone walking right in front of the lens. True story. I wish I was exaggerating.

It was only when I melted the label of a fizzy drink through the bottle, that we were finally asked to leave. But by then, we had our footage – and the rain had, at last, stopped.

It had been fun, but I couldn't help but feel that we had wasted our time. I begrudgingly edited the footage on my laptop and exported a final version: a fairly rough video – all filmed on an iPhone 6, three minutes long and patched together with some cheesy, royalty-free music slapped on top. We called it 'Magic in Tesco'. Creative title.

'Put that on Facebook!' suggested Kymann.

I *never* posted on Facebook. But once again, being outnumbered, I did what I was told. And as I expected, Kymann was wrong. The video didn't get thousands of views.

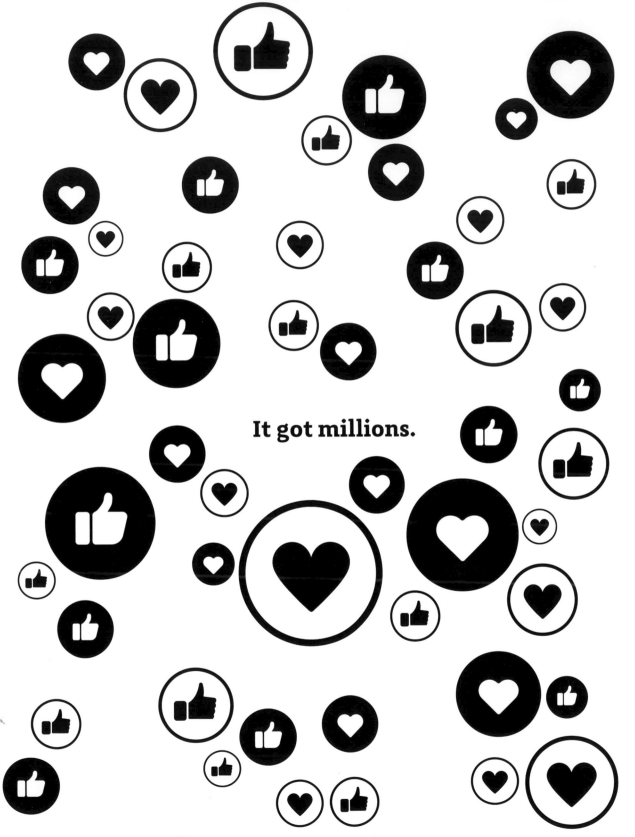

It got millions.

I couldn't believe it – for the first time in my life, I was getting some real attention online!

Within two days, the video had 3 million views. Within a week, it had over 7 million. I know, I know, compared to the numbers other social media entertainers get, that isn't mind-blowing – but to me, that was 7 million more views than I had ever had.

I remember refreshing the Facebook page over and over, and watching my page jump from 700 people, to almost 15,000 overnight. Again, not massive numbers in the grand scheme of things, but for me, that was staggering.

And so my first viral video was born. Time to make another. After some *serious meetings*, we decided to go for 'Magic in McDonald's'. Yet another astoundingly creative title.

The McDonald's video was much better. Better tricks, better preparation, better everything. Except for my haircut. That got dramatically worse. (Check it out for yourself. Warning, the haircut may cause some readers to feel nauseous.)

The final product looked great, but it was a brutal experience. Twelve hours involving, among other things, Shane having to lie on a greasy floor for what felt like for ever. I remember him looking up at me and saying, 'Joel – I'm thirty, I'm married, I own an apartment and here I am on the floor of McDonald's, trying to make a chicken nugget appear. What has my life come to?' Love you, man.

As for me, attempting to pull off 'the replenishing burger' illusion, I must have eaten at least fifteen cheeseburgers.

I couldn't eat fast food for months afterwards, scarred by the aftertaste.

I'd love to say that the video smashed it – but it didn't. It bombed. Didn't even come close to the initial success of 'Magic in Tesco'.

Nor did the following video, 'Hotel Magic'. Although as much as 'Hotel Magic' wasn't successful, it was a *dream* to film compared to the others. I think we all just needed an excuse to make a trip to the spa after our previous filming experiences.

With a feeling in my gut that what I was doing would eventually work, I pushed through the failures, time and time again, until finally, it did. If there is one thing I've learned, both from experience and from other incredibly successful content creators, it's that the skill to develop, above all others, is persistence.

Since 'Magic in Tesco', I've posted over 800 videos, and I imagine at the time of going to press, that number will be considerably higher. Were all those videos good? Nope. Are some of them good? For sure.

The key is to keep going, even when things look hopeless. You're only one video away from potentially changing your life. So don't hang around like I did, waiting for permission from others to put yourself out there.

Looking back, I wish I had started believing in myself and setting bigger goals sooner. I always had the skewed belief that others could accomplish things, but I couldn't – that success and dreams were meant for other people, but not for me. I have long since abandoned this useless, self-limiting belief. I suggest that you do the same.

It's very easy to be discouraged when beginning your journey towards social media success. It can feel pointless to start filming a video when no one is watching. And believe me, even when people are watching it can be difficult to build up the enthusiasm to get in front of a camera.

Which is why it's so important to focus on what you want, and not on your current circumstances. Where you are right now has nothing to do with where you're going to be. So don't let the present dictate your future. Because remember, the next piece of content you post could open up all sorts of doors for you. It could change your life.

One day I was feeling particularly drained and tired, having spent the night before streaming online. I was not in the mood to jump in front of the camera, let alone begin editing a video or all the other tasks that come with creating social media content.

But having heard the advice 'your next video could be the one that changes your life' from somebody (I honestly can't remember who), I got started.

I filmed a twenty-second video with my brother, performing what I felt was a very basic magic trick. I thought so little of it that I barely remembered to post it, and only did so right before I fell asleep, just before midnight.

When I woke up, that basic video had reached 20 million people. More views than I had ever experienced before! And I wouldn't have made it, had I not realised that my next video might actually be the big one.

Of course, this doesn't mean you should just throw out any old nonsense online. That's not my point. My point is that although things may get strenuous or even challenging, you never know what might be right around the corner. So don't give up when you might be just about to hit gold. Keep going.

EXTERNAL FORCES

Get set for some more trick tok tips to set you firmly on the path to online majesty and glory.

FOCUS ON THE THINGS YOU CAN CONTROL

A really important piece of advice I'd like to give to every single content creator out there is this: don't attach your self-worth and happiness to things that are outside of your control.

Of course, this applies to everything in life, but it's particularly important to remember if your goal is to grow a brand online. I've seen people literally crippled with anxiety over a week of bad social views. And I understand why – but over time, I've learned not to let it affect me.

Let's imagine you nail a video, and it gets 100 million views. Awesome! But then your next video only gets, say, 100,000. If you attach your self-esteem, your confidence and your intelligence to 100 million, then how are you going to feel at 100,000? Are you going to feel one thousand times more stupid?

That sounds extreme, but I've seen it happen. I've had friends in tears over a drop in social media fame. It's all too easy to get wrapped up in the numbers. It's an addictive game. But it's an unhealthy way to live.

There are so many factors outside of your control that go into a viral video. I've had the same video get 10 million views on one platform and 10,000 on another. The same video. Although there are a lot of things you can do to increase your

chances of success (all the tips I gave you on pages 66–79), there are so many moving parts on social media platforms that it's silly to try and control outcomes.

So don't focus on that. Instead, focus all your attention on what you can control: your thoughts and your actions.

Improve your videos, make more videos, do whatever it takes, but realise that even then, there is still a major element of luck to the game. All you can do is keep going, stay persistent and don't let a negative result knock you off track.

I'll be honest – there was a period of time when I was getting some videos stopping at around the 100,000-view mark, and for me, that was low. It was frustrating, and I let it get to me. How ridiculous! I know people who would have chopped off their arm for that number of views.

So keep things in perspective, understand that number chasing, although important for growth, should never be something that ruins more than a moment of your day.

BE YOURSELF (AND THEN SOME)

We've all been told 'just be yourself.' It's good advice, and I wish I had stopped trying to be other people far sooner, and really leaned into what makes me me. The moment I did, people started paying more attention.

Your biggest asset is you. There is no one quite like you, and that alone is a massive selling point. I get it – when starting out, we all emulate heroes and idols. That's natural. But at some point, you've got to stretch out and be you. People will love you for it.

Having said that, there is a caveat.

Be yourself, but don't be boring. Who you are right now, is not the best version of you. Always strive to be more entertaining, more interesting and more charismatic – at least on camera!

I'm not suggesting being superficial or fake; I'm saying you should always aim to be improving in every area of your life. If you *can* be better, *be* better. And make sure to show up as your best self on camera.

Equally as important, however, is to be real. Don't put on a character that doesn't reflect who you truly are. You'll never be the best by trying to be someone else. It'll become exhausting, and they've already beaten you to it anyway. Be yourself, and always seek out ways to become better.

I WAS FOOLED — BADLY!

As a magician, it's my job to entertain and amuse, but most importantly, to confuse. (Except when creating content! See pages 66–79.)

No matter which way you try to swing it, magicians fool people. Ideally, we do that in a way that is fun, mysterious and engaging, but at the end of the day, if we don't fool you, the magic isn't all that impressive.

As such, I've got very used to the feeling of disorientating people. So much so that these days, I sometimes have to put myself into the shoes of the spectator, in order to remind myself of how cool the magic I perform must be for someone experiencing it for the first time.

When you first get into magic, it's not uncommon to feel a sense of guilt when performing. After all, the secrets are often so simple and so obvious once you see behind the curtain that it can make you feel fraudulent, getting so much admiration for something so trivial. But that's part of the act, and if you downplay someone else's amazement, you're stripping them of the joy that they're experiencing. It would be criminal to ruin that feeling of pure incredulity by underplaying the wonder of the trick. And so the right thing to do is to allow yourself to keep the secret and essentially lie to the spectator. After all, it's a lie that will bring them more happiness. So if ever I feel that twinge of guilt after pulling off some mythical stunt, I try to recapture the feeling I had when watching that magician levitate a red sponge ball all those years ago. And I remember that ignorance is bliss.

I can relate heavily to a scene in the wonderful tale of 'The Red-Headed League', one of my favourite Sherlock Holmes stories, in which our hero has just deduced something absolutely astonishing about a client

he has never met before and the client, in turn, is absolutely astonished, in a way that is similar to someone who may have witnessed a magic trick. Holmes, unable to help himself, divulges his deductive process to the client. Upon finding out how he arrived at his conclusions, the client remarks, 'I thought at first that you had done something clever, but I see that there was nothing in it, after all'.

While there are times when exposing the method behind a trick can be more entertaining than the trick itself – Penn and Teller's cups-and-balls routine is a perfect example of this – for the most part, keeping the secret is the best way forward. As Alfred Borden (Christian Bale's character in the fantastic movie *The Prestige*) puts it, having blown a child's mind by making a coin appear: 'Never show anyone. They'll beg you and flatter you for the secret, but the second you give it up, you'll be nothing to them.'

At any rate, I've become very comfortable withholding information from the average person. Half of being a magician is being able to convincingly lie to someone's face and feel no guilt. And, as such, I've become quite intuitive over the years, and can usually tell when someone else is fibbing. So much so that a couple of my favourite routines on stage are based around lie detection. I'll have people join me on stage, ask them to think of two truths and a lie, and with almost 100 per cent accuracy, tell them which is the truth, and which is a pile of nonsense.

Or maybe that's a lie. I'll let you decide!

This sort of thing is only really possible when I'm with someone in person, over the phone, or via handwriting. And so I have to confess that I, the hoodwinker, was hoodwinked.

To this day, this is still the most unusual, and bizarre thing that's happened to me when it comes to operating an entertainment business.

I was twenty-one-years old, and had started to take social media seriously. I hadn't experienced much success, but at the same time, we'd occasionally get enquiries in about brand work or promoting products online. Almost all of them led to nothing or weren't a good fit. But now and then, something would come in that seemed like a really cool opportunity. This was one of those cases.

Back then, I was using Facebook quite a lot, primarily to stay in touch with family and friends. I was on the app when I realised I had a message request, so I took a look, expecting it to be some form of spam or someone I hadn't spoken to in a while. I was not expecting a business request. I mean, who reaches out to a private Facebook account for a business enquiry? Apparently, Mia Anderson. Hmmm, Mia Anderson. What an interesting human being.

Mia's FB page was private, so I couldn't see any details about her, but at the same time, everything looked fairly legitimate. Her account was linked to an Instagram page, her profile picture looked dated, but normal and she even listed some previous work experience.

Her message read as follows:

> Hi Joel, Mia Anderson here. We're looking for a magician to create a bespoke illusion for an upcoming corporate event, and we think you would be a perfect fit. Do you think you could accomplish something similar to this?

She dropped a link to a YouTube video featuring, hands down, the worst magic trick I've ever seen. Ever. I mean, truly awful. Worse than my jokes.

The trick was essentially a man standing in his laundry room holding a massive black cloak in front of his body. By some devilry, a sock appeared just above the cloak, and danced around. The sock then ducked behind the cloak, and then reappeared. The same thing happened over and over for three minutes. Worst of all, you could easily tell how the trick was done. No hate to the magician in the video (although thinking about it, I doubt he actually was a magician), but serious hate to anyone who watched it and thought, 'that's a good idea, let's do that'.

I'm a pretty honest person. (At least, I'm honest about my dishonesty.) I'll tell you if I think something is bad. And I expect the same of everyone who meets me. So I replied to Mia:

> Mia, thanks for reaching out. I'm delighted that you think I'd be a fit for this event, and I can assure you that I can accomplish something similar to that shown in that video. Personally, I don't think that trick is any good. If I were to do the same thing, I'd spend time making it more deceptive, and somewhat fooling! Is there a particular reason as to why you've chosen that trick?

I also asked for more details about the event, but, to be honest, I was really perplexed as to why someone would want their event to feature such an unusual spectacle.

Mia got back to me, thrilled that I could accomplish something even better than the initial video. She gave me more details, explaining that the event was for a sports company, which I won't name. The idea was to do the sock illusion, but with a sports sock, manufactured by that brand. Now it made more sense.

Hating the concept of the trick, I suggested multiple alternative sock-related illusions, but Mia assured me that this was what the client wanted. And it was at this point that things started to get moving. Mia asked if I could put together a routine and send across video footage of me performing the trick; or, at the very least, send across my suggested method to make the trick better. Usually, I wouldn't disclose a routine's secret to a client, but this was such a niche request that I saw no harm in giving away my proposed method.

I had decided that to make the trick work, and look good, I would need a bunch of different things. Firstly, I'd need a custom-made jacket that allowed my arm to slip in and out of the sleeve, under the cover of the cloak. I'd also need a silicone hand – a replica of my own, complete with rings just like mine. I spent some serious time putting this method together and then sent it across to Mia. This was when her questions started rolling in.

I have never in my life been so interrogated by someone. Mia left no stone unturned, grilling me over the tiniest details of how the trick would operate. I was happy to answer, though, as the company in question was colossal, and I really wanted the gig.

But the questions were really specialised, covering things I hadn't even considered. 'What colour will the lining of the jacket be? Will you have magnets inside the inner shell of the fake arm?' Things I would have imagined no client would care about, just as long as the result was guaranteed. And it got to a point where the questions were coming at me so thick and fast and were so specific, that it was actually beginning to feel like hard work. Which, of course, is fine, but I wasn't prepared to put all this work in, only for her to choose another magician using all of my ideas.

So I asked that before any more information on the trick was discussed, a contract was drawn up, confirming me as the magician for the event, and for us to discuss my fees.

This was when my mind was blown. I had figured that the budget for this sort of event would be large, but I wasn't prepared for the fee they offered. I won't give a specific number, because it will be astronomical to some readers, and chicken feed to others. But for me, the proposed fee was more money than I had received from all my previous work in magic put together. It would have increased my bank balance tenfold.

As someone starting out in the world of showbiz, I was absolutely shocked. And excited. And nervous. All the classic adrenaline-fuelled emotions hit me at once. I was prepared to do anything to lock in this job.

So the contract was drawn up, and the work was detailed as being one performance at this company event, alongside a few social media posts promoting the new sports product that was being launched. Score. My managers and I looked over the deal and went for it. We signed the contract, and I got ready to work.

The event was to be in November, and at the time of signing the contract it was May. So plenty of time to prepare and master the routine. I started working on the props needed for the trick, ordering jackets, magnets, invisible threads and all sorts of other materials. I even brought in a professional SFX artist to make the custom replica hand. Things were moving forward, and I couldn't have been happier.

A couple of weeks went by, as I continued to correspond with Mia. She was delighted that everything was going well and dropped in the occasional question or request, while every couple of days, I would send a video message, showing advancements with the props and new ideas to make the routine better.

August came. It was the fourteenth, my birthday. I'm not a birthday person – at least not at this point in my life. I guess I've always seen my birthday as one big reminder that I'm running out of time. Depressing. And no matter how I try to reframe that thought, I always end up thinking that way. I can't help it.

I like cake, though!

So as per usual, I hadn't planned anything major for my birthday. Instead, I had invited my friends Shane and Kymann to travel from Dublin to Belfast and hang out for the day.

Now, I perform mentalism. *I'm* meant to be the one who influences *others'* decisions and thoughts. But somehow, by some method unknown to me, my girlfriend had convinced me to invite the boys down and forget that it hadn't been my own decision. It wasn't my choice. She had actually planned on them being there to distract me from

. . . wait for it . . . my surprise party. And I really was surprised. I guess I can't tell when *everyone* is lying to me, after all.

So while Lucy was busy getting her house prepared for the big surprise, Shane and Kymann kept me busy, taking me to a hotel in Belfast where we celebrated not only my birthday, but also the big gig that I had landed.

And it was only then, sitting down and really thinking about the event, that I noticed how weird the situation actually was. For the first time since reading Mia's initial message, I felt doubt creep in. I don't know what it was – maybe I was just bummed out because it was my birthday – but I was suddenly seeing it all differently. I voiced this to the two guys, and they both agreed that the whole thing was fishy, but we were likely overthinking it.

Nevertheless, in a split second, I had made up my mind that the entire thing had to be a scam. I felt it in my bones. And so, in that very moment, I pulled out my phone and sent a message to Mia:

> Hi Mia, I've put together all of the necessary props for the illusion, and everything is ready to go. We're well ahead of schedule! I'll send across a complete video of the routine in action this coming Monday. Can I ask that you take a look at my expenses attached, and see that I am reimbursed for the cost of materials? Many thanks!

I already knew that I wasn't going to be reimbursed. I don't know how – I just did. And I was right. A week went by and I heard nothing; then two, then three.

After deciding the thing was a hoax, we looked again at the contract. We realised, upon closer inspection, that some subtle discrepancies made the agreement invalid. Nightmare.

Thankfully, I hadn't been dumb enough to actually tell many people about the gig. That would have been mortifying. Instead, I was just disappointed, and felt like I had wasted a lot of my time. Which I suppose I had.

But no matter how many people I spoke to about the whole situation, nobody could figure out why any of it had happened at all. Was Mia merely trying to waste my time? Or was it something bigger than that?

I had my own theory. I believed that Mia was another magician who really had been offered a similar job and wanted to use my magic expertise to improve the routine without having to pay a consultancy fee. It made sense to me and most people who heard my theory agreed with it.

I should not have thought so little of my fellow magicians, however, for this was not the case, as you'll soon discover.

Christmas arrived, and the alleged November corporate event had long passed. Naturally, it had never existed; we did our research, albeit too late.

I was performing at a Christmas party, when I felt my phone vibrate in my pocket. I checked to see the notification. It was a Facebook message . . . and it was from Mia Anderson. I couldn't believe my eyes.

Hi Joel, apologies for the delayed response! The event was postponed due to outside circumstances, but now we're all set to go for an event in March. Can you have the routine ready for then? Wishing you a very merry Christmas!

Christmas probably would have been a lot more entertaining for me and my family had my fee for that gig not been fake, but regardless, I was amazed that Mia was no longer, well, MIA.

Fully aware that this was a scam, I decided to get to the bottom of it. I was over the disappointment and now just wanted answers. So I decided to play dumb and get the conversation going again. Only this time, I was sure to avoid any talk of payment, wanting to see how far I could take things.

Events unfolded in almost exactly the same way as before – new contract, new date, same sock-puppet routine. In all the new conversations, I didn't really learn anything. But I did have some fun coming up with ludicrous methods for the sock-puppet trick, even suggesting we build a robot arm and attach it to me, Doctor-Octopus-style. She seemed thrilled by the outlandish ideas, which told me that I wasn't speaking to an undercover magician. Theory blown.

Then, with only one week to go before the event, when I asked about travel to the 'venue', she ghosted me again. So Mia Anderson had pulled her own magic trick and disappeared. I wouldn't hear from her again.

Eventually, the whole ordeal left my mind and I moved on with my life. Eight months went by.

I was in London, working on my TV show, *Ultimate Magic Skills*. This was right in the middle of Covid-19, so I was isolating in an apartment in Shoreditch before filming began.

Luckily for me, I wasn't filming the show on my own, and my good friend Tom – my co-star in the show – was isolating with me, after all sorts of logistical nightmares caused by the pandemic.

Because we couldn't leave the apartment, we spent a good deal of time talking. Over dinner one night (may I add, the best dinner I've ever had. Dim sum in central London, yes please), we got on to the topic of work.

For both of us, things had changed very suddenly, as all live shows had been cancelled due to the pandemic, so any talk of them was unusual.

'Did I tell you about the gig I just landed?' Tom said to me, stuffing a duck spring roll into his mouth.

I was intrigued. A live show, right in the middle of a pandemic? No chance.

'No! What's the deal?' I asked.

'It's a strange one, mate. I've to create a routine all about a sock. Got the gig on Instagram.'

'No. Way. Who is the contact?' I already knew the answer before I asked.

'Mia Anderson.'

So she was back in action, and this time taking on Tom. I proceeded to tell him the same story that I've just told you, and of course, he was shocked, but also delighted that he hadn't spent any time on it yet.

We decided that we needed to get the bottom of the situation. Sure, she hadn't caused much harm in the end when it came to me and Tom, but for all we knew, she could be reaching out to younger or less investigative magicians and taking advantage.

I called Shane and told him what had happened. He agreed with Tom and me and, concerned that somewhere, somehow, someone was going to get hurt if Mia wasn't stopped, he developed a plan.

Shane asked Tom to move the conversation with Mia from Instagram to email. That way, we'd be able to get hold of her email address and, with any luck, track the domain. Once we had that, Shane got to work. And what we found, was ridiculous.

It was my dad the entire time.

Kidding. But what a twist that would have been!

For real: Shane did some digging and it turns out, we were right. The whole thing was a scam, obviously, but in a bigger way than we expected.

You see, Mia Anderson wasn't *just* Mia Anderson. The IP address associated with that email was being called out left, right and centre for attempting – and succeeding – in many online scams. Thousands of pounds' worth of damage. I'm not exactly sure how Mia had planned on getting my money, but I wasn't prepared to find out; so we reported the incident online and to our fellow magicians, so that they, too, could avoid being hoodwinked.

And of course, Tom dodged the scam, too. Lucky for both of us! And although it did waste a lot of my time, mental energy and some nice denim jackets, I learned a valuable lesson: don't over hype something until it's happened. I wish I had learned this sooner. Incredible things may happen to you in your life, but you will also experience some setbacks. People will back out of promises, and things won't go as planned. So don't make it harder on yourself by getting prematurely excited about projects that might not ever happen. Do your due diligence, check everything and, most importantly, if someone called Mia Anderson drops you a message – let me know!

SCAM ANYONE!
(I WAS FOOLED!)

Short on cash? I got you.

No, I'm not suggesting that I'll lend you my hard-earned pennies, but what I've got for you is even better. As they say, give a man a fish, and you'll feed him for a day; teach a man to fish and you feed him for a lifetime.

Well, I can't fish, but I can give you the secret to a little scam that will, time and time again, deliver you any amount of collateral that you desire.

I'm not saying that *I* use this scam – but that doesn't mean you can't give it a try.

Of course, I jest. Because although what I'm about to teach you is a fantastic ploy that could easily generate endless cash, I recommend you use it purely for entertainment. (Unless you happen to stumble across Mia Anderson, in which case you could use this trick to give her a taste of her own medicine.)

THE TRICK

Here's what happens:

- Removing a pack of cards from your pocket (no one else had a pack on them), you hand the pasteboards (cards) to the nearest individual and ask them to thoroughly shuffle and examine them.

- Taking the cards back, show them around, making it clear that they are all, in fact, different and, more importantly, randomised.

- After spreading the cards face down on the table, ask the spectator to choose one and take a look at it, without showing you. Like Spiderman, the card's identity must remain a secret.

- The card is placed back inside the deck by the spectator, and you offer them the chance to cut the cards as many times as they desire, ensuring that their card is lost.

- 'I'm going to read your mind,' you say next. 'Well, to be honest, I'm going to read your facial expressions. In a moment, I'm going to deal through these cards, and when I do, without telling me anything, you're going to give away what your card is. I'm just going to get a sense for it. So try not to give away too much. Make this difficult for me.'

- You begin to deal the shuffled cards to the table, face up. Studying the expression of the spectator intensely, you continue to deal, until you stop at a seemingly random spot.

- You say: 'I bet you £10 that the next card I turn over is your card. Should I get this wrong, I'll give you the money. But if the next card I turn over truly is your card, would you give me £10 in return, for blowing your mind?'

- The spectator instantly takes the bet. Not because they doubt your skills, but because they can clearly see that their card has already been dealt down to the table, and that you whizzed past it, without blinking an eye. The next card to be dealt therefore, could not be theirs. They would be mad not to take the £10.

- You begin to turn over the next card, but then pause, set down the remaining cards and stare into the eyes of the spectator. Reaching down, you take their card from the dealt pile and flip it over.

Mic. Drop.

The spectator is a student, so doesn't have £10 – instead they offer to clean your car. And you are a magician, so you don't have a car. They each face the reality of their respective crippling financial situations and spend the rest of the night in tears.

THE SECRET

So how does one pull off this little scam? Well, the secret is simple, but the thing that makes this con so effective is the wordplay used to convince the spectator that they cannot lose.

And what's particularly fantastic about this trick is that it's actually better when you're not a magician. When I perform this, people are on the defensive, expecting me to get their card right, watching out for any form of trickery. But if you're not a magician – or, at least, the spectators don't know you to be one – you'll get even greater results and reactions with this.

All you need to pull it off is one piece of secret knowledge: the key card principle.

What is the key card principle, you ask? Well, let's assume that somebody has picked a playing card, and you don't know what it is. In order to find out, all you need to know is the identity of the card beside it. If you know that, you can use it as a 'key' to deduce the chosen card.

Let's break down the method, step by step:

- Give the cards to a spectator and ask them to shuffle them. The cards are genuinely mixed, and unprepared.

- Take the cards back and display them in a way that everyone can see the faces, pointing out that 'all the cards are different'. Really, you're using this sentence as a justification to **remember the bottom card**.

The bottom card is your *key card*. Remember it at all costs.

- Turn the deck face down and invite the spectator to choose a card at random. Ask them to keep it hidden from you. While they are looking at it, lift about half the cards from the top and place them on the table.

- Ask the spectator to place their card on top of the pile on the table. Then simply drop the remaining cards on top. Can you see what's just happened? You've now effectively placed their chosen card beneath your key card (see photos 9 and 10).

- Invite the spectator to cut the cards as many times as they'd like. You may be thinking, But Joel, won't that mess up the order and separate the key card from the chosen card?

No, it won't.

You see, a deck of cards is a cyclical stack. Meaning, that as long as you cut the cards and put them back together again, the actual order doesn't change, merely the start and end point.

If you don't believe me, put a deck of cards in a new order, and perform as many complete cuts as you'd like. When you're done, notice that all the cards are still in the same order – just the top and bottom ones have changed. One selective cut of the cards, and they'll be back to normal.

- Tell the spectator that you're going to read their facial expressions and use them to guess which card they're thinking of. Begin dealing the cards to the table in a way that they can all be seen. As you do this, act as though you're attempting to pick up on their body language. All you actually *have to do* is keep a keen eye out for your key card.

- The moment you see the key, you know, with 100 per cent accuracy, that the next card you deal down will be their card. But don't stop. Keep dealing, just keep a strong mental note of what their card is. You're already a step ahead of them. Keep dealing for as long as you like, then, at some point, stop.

- Place your bet. Tell the spectator that you bet (however much you'd like) that the next card you turn over will be their card. The wording is important. You see, you've just conditioned them to seeing cards being turned over, and over, so they're now expecting you to turn over *the next card in the remaining pile*.

- Assuming they take the bet (which they always do), act as though you're about to turn over the next card in the pile. Then, hesitate, put down the pile and flip over their chosen card.

Bask in the glorious frustration of your opponent.

So there we have it. A stupendous scam that you can utilise either to entertain or to drain the pockets of others.

PS I take no responsibility for any £10 notes seized unlawfully.

Now for some notes. There are only a few things that could go wrong when doing this, so be on the lookout for them:

1. The spectator cuts the cards incorrectly. Make sure that when you offer them the chance to cut the cards, you demonstrate a perfect, complete cut. That means lifting off a cluster and putting the bottom half back on top. If the spectator decides to go crazy and split the cards into nineteen *different* piles and then pile them up again in a different order, it'll likely separate the key card from their chosen card.

2. You forget the key card. When you look at the bottom card, commit it to memory. Repeat it in your head three times if necessary. Also – and this sounds silly – make sure to flip over *their chosen card* when it comes to the reveal, not your key card. I've seen people forget which is which and lose the bet!

3. The key card ends up on the top or bottom of the pack. This happens every so often, but if so, don't panic. If you deal through the cards and the first one is the key card, that just means that their card is second. And if the key card is on the bottom of the deck (i.e. the final card you deal), then it means their card was the first you dealt. In that case, I'd suggest pretending that you couldn't guess their card, pick up the deck, shuffle them and start dealing again. It won't happen often, but best to be prepared.

4. The spectator lies about which card they chose. This does happen, especially if there is money on the line. So how do we get around it? Simply ask the spectator to show their card to the audience when they choose it. This will ensure that they are honest.

1.

2.

3.

4.

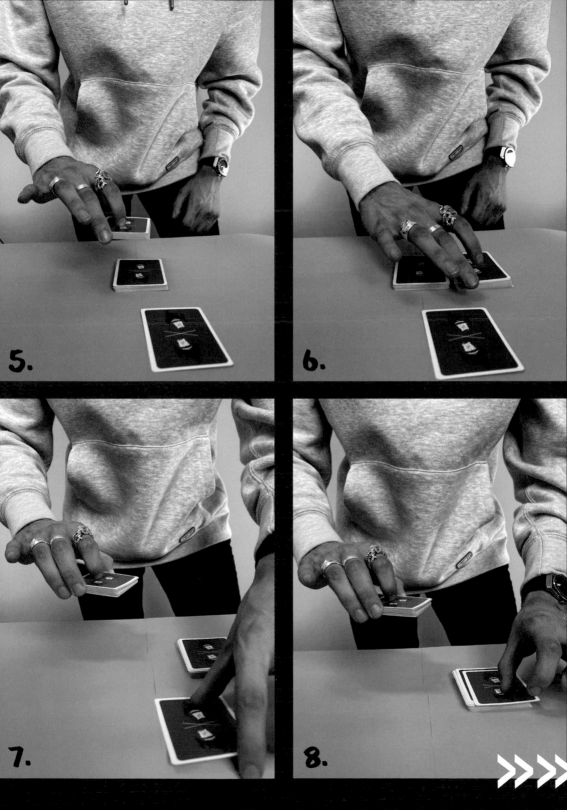

5.

6.

7.

8.

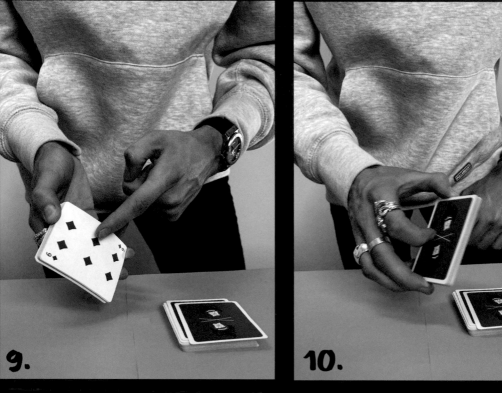

13.

14.

15.

16.

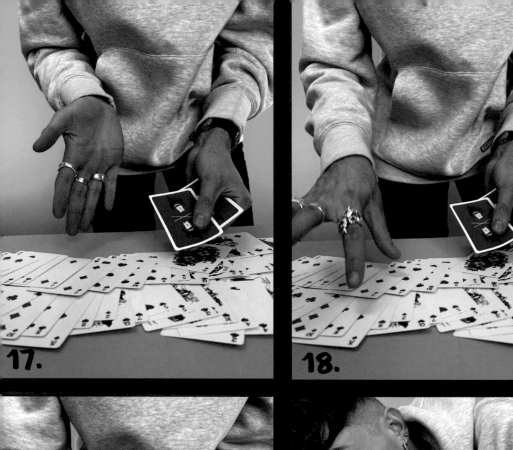

17.

18.

19.

20.

You can tell when something's going wrong for me on stage because it's the only time I sweat. This story is a brilliant – and sticky – example of that.

You may remember that we talked about the fact that magic doesn't always go to plan. Of course, the real beauty of magic is that nobody really knows which direction it might go in. And this gives the magician freedom to make some mistakes and, hopefully, to rectify them.

Any magician who tells you they don't get tricks wrong is lying. But who can blame them? I mean, let's face it, magicians lie for a living. Come to think of it, there are quite a few jobs like that, but let's not go there . . .

When you begin practising magic, now and again you'll drop a coin, expose some sleight of hand or make any number of rookie mistakes – and that's just fine. You can't expect to be perfect right off the bat.

But you see, as the illusions get bigger, and the crowd gets larger, making a mistake is more costly. Especially if you're being paid.

I've already told you about the time I made an engagement ring disappear – almost for good. That was mortifying, of course, but at least in that case, I was just a kid, so mistakes were to be expected.

The same cannot be said for the time I messed up the finale to a show, in front of a thousand people. At the age of twenty-one.

Get ready . . . this one's a doozy.

To add some context, it's worth adding that by the time I was twenty-one, I had a lot of stage experience, relative to my age. I mention that because making this mistake was borderline inexcusable. It's something that I would have expected a three-year-old child to get right.

I love performing at all sorts of events, but my favourite role, without a doubt, is being the MC. The pressure of holding an event together gives me a massive adrenaline rush, keeping me on my toes and, as an extra bonus, you get to meet all sorts of wonderful people. It's not easy work, although the best MCs do make it look easy.

So . . . I was twenty-one, and had just been asked to host a massive event – by far, the biggest I had ever been booked for and a really great opportunity for me. Ecstatic would be an understatement! I remember receiving the enquiry email and quite literally punching the air.

All my life, I had been looking forward to a time when I would be on a stage, entertaining large groups of people. And that time had finally arrived. Of course, I had hosted lots of other wonderful events, but they had always been much, much smaller. Less pressure, for sure. But now, the years of hard work and perseverance had paid off, and here was my chance to show my worth. So I took the booking, marked it in my calendar and started to prepare.

When I host events, it's a mash of introducing others to the stage and announcing house rules, but also, of course, performing magic. That's my USP over other hosts. When the event starts to get dull – perhaps a previous speaker has gone on for a few minutes too long – I jump in to raise the energy in the room.

When the day of the event finally arrived, I was feeling confident that I was well prepared, and ready to give it my very best. Mic on, stage set . . . and action!

It's always funny to see the look on some of the faces of slightly older people in the crowd when they realise their host for the evening could quite possibly be the same age as one of their grandchildren. But they usually get on board after the opening trick.

I kicked off the evening by inviting a very respectable-looking gent to the stage. Moments later, a full pint glass of water was levitating above his head. Don't worry, this trick didn't go wrong. (Although it has gone wrong for me in the past – I will never forget the moment a full glass of champagne decided to stop levitating, just as it was hovering over the head of a young lady who had clearly dressed up for the occasion. She was not pleased. But hey, at least it wasn't red wine.)

Moments before I accidentally dropped the glass of water all over this poor girl's head . . .

In any case, the trick went perfectly and the crowd was now fully engaged. It was all going just the way I had planned: my jokes were landing, the speakers appreciated my warm introductions and all my interlude tricks were going down a storm – which made me extra excited, as my final trick was going to be on another level altogether.

Throughout the evening, I was constantly thinking about the finale. I had brought my A-game – a trick that I knew, if it worked, could be a reputation maker. It was my favourite trick to perform in the limelight: the newspaper prediction.

If you happened to catch my first television show, *Life is Magic*, you'll have seen this trick for yourself. It's the type that not only fools laypeople, but also fries magicians from time to time. It is so close to being perfect that I've barely changed it since the first time I performed it, many years ago.

Let me break it down for you. Before the show begins, I take a daily newspaper and choose an interesting word. That word acts as my prediction, my target, and once I've chosen it, I write it down on a scroll. And nobody, besides me, knows what is written inside it. The scrolls vary in size, depending on the scale of the show, but in this case it was huge, covering the entire breadth of the stage.

Hanging in full view above the stage, from the moment the audience enter the auditorium, the scroll never leaves anyone's sight. In fact, I encourage audience members to take it in turns when leaving for bathroom breaks, so that I never get the chance to mess with it.

This is the exact set-up I used for this very special performance. A 20-foot scroll, hanging above the stage – a visual enigma, a constant reminder that there is another spectacle to come. And with this set-up in place, I was ready to perform my finale.

The evening was about to come to an end, and it was time for me to wrap things up with one final miracle trick.

Or so I thought.

'Ladies and gentlemen, you've been such a wonderful audience tonight, so I thought I'd leave you with something special,' I said. 'If this goes as planned, it's something you'll be telling people about for years and years. Tonight, we're going to predict the future.'

Bold, right? Quite the promise. But with a trick this strong, you can afford to make such grandiose claims.

The trick begins with about fifty newspapers being distributed around the room. I ask volunteers to do this, so that everything is random. And the newspapers are real. No funny business.

The next step is for an audience member to join me on stage. They are to be the star of the show, selected using the paper-ball method described earlier to ensure a truly random choice.

In this case, a lovely lady was chosen to play the main part. She stood up and held the paper ball tightly in her hands.

'Madame, before you join me on stage, could I ask you to name the first colour that pops into your mind please?'

'Blue.'

'Interesting that you chose blue,' I said. 'And that felt like a free choice?' 'Yes, of course.'

'And you could have chosen any colour at all . . . why don't you open up that paper ball and read what it says aloud?'

The lady did as instructed, only to find scrawled upon the crumpled paper in bold marker:

YOU WILL SAY THE COLOUR BLUE

'We've found a psychic!' I exclaimed. 'Please welcome this lovely lady to the stage!'

Everything was going to plan. I had found the perfect volunteer, the audience were on my side and the scroll, hanging above me, was about to knock them dead.

And that was when things started to go ever so slightly wrong. Not to mention exceedingly messy, as – with dozens of newspapers distributed around the room – I was about to cause carnage.

'I need everyone to listen very carefully. Because without every single one of you taking part, this may not work,' I said. 'For about thirty seconds, I need you all to abandon any sense of being responsible and go crazy. Unleash your inner, ignored maniac.

'As I count down from thirty, I want those newspapers to be mixed up as far as humanly possible. Shred them, throw them . . . do whatever you want to them. Just make sure that when I get to zero, you still have some paper in your hands. Make sense? OK. GO!'

I always love this part of the show. As expected, the room went into total pandemonium. Newspaper was being thrown around at a rate faster than I could have possibly expected. It was

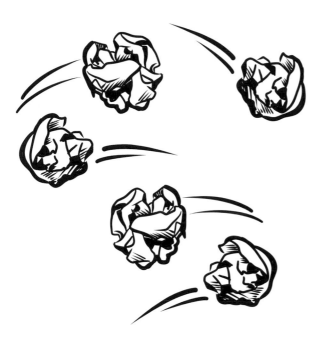

Remember the gigantic scroll, hanging above the stage? Of course you do. Well, I suddenly became aware that I couldn't remember the word I'd written on it.

Mind. Blank. Not a hope of remembering. And the whole finale of the show depended on me knowing that word. You can see my problem.

glorious. Although usually, I perform this trick for an audience of around fifty people, never a thousand. So there was total chaos all around. (To all the people over the years who have helped me clean up the aftermath of this illusion, my spine thanks you.)

'Three . . . two . . . one . . . stop!'

The audience was eventually restored to a semi-controlled state, with everyone in the room eagerly holding a fistful of paper. And my job now was to make the lady on stage choose the correct piece of paper, the right sentence and, eventually, the predicted word. All while giving the impression that she had free choice. Another normal day at the office.

At this point, I'd already performed this trick a hundred times and had absolute confidence in myself and the method. So it shouldn't have been a challenge at all.

Slight issue.

It was at this precise moment that the sweat began to break out on my forehead. A solid indicator – for someone who almost never sweats on stage – that something has gone badly wrong.

So let's take a look at my situation:

I'm standing on stage, in front of a thousand people. Up until this point, everything has gone perfectly. It's my job to bring the evening to a climactic end. I've hyped up audience expectations, but I'm now clueless as to how I'm supposed to end the show. Just then . . .

. . . the word jumped right back inside my head, amid a rush of almighty relief.

Excellent.

That was the word. I remembered it vividly, and my confidence levels burst through the roof instantly. I was ready to finish the show. One last hurrah.

I asked the lady on stage to make a series of decisions, gradually eliminating every piece of newspaper in the room until she was happy with just one. Incredibly fair. She then chose a paragraph on that page. Then a sentence. And then, finally, a single word.

'Madame, out of all the words in all the newspapers in this room, which would you like to choose? It's your choice.'

'Excellent.'

I had done it. I had psychologically nudged her into choosing precisely the right word. And to her (and the 999 spectators in the room), it was a genuinely random free choice.

Now it was time to reveal my prediction.

'Madame, would you please be so kind as to gently pull down that scroll that's hanging above your head? Be very careful that no one tries to touch it or switch it out for something else. Perfect. Now hold on to that end because, in a moment, we're going to open this up for everyone to see.'

You could hear a pin drop. Everyone's attention was focused on the scroll.

'Ladies and gentlemen – fifty newspapers. One thousand people. Hundreds of thousands of words. You controlled every action. Should one of you have moved a single sheet of newspaper in a different direction, we would have ended up with a different piece on stage. Meaning that any one of an infinite number of words could have been selected. But tonight, the chosen word was?'

'Excellent,' said the lady, with a look on her face that clearly said: no way.

I dragged out every second. Prepared to milk the moment for all it was worth.

'Ladies and gentlemen, I have been Joel M, you have been absolutely wonderful!'

And in a dramatic flourish, I opened the scroll to its full extent, held my other arm high in the air and exclaimed, 'Goodnight!'

Silence.

My goodness, they're speechless, I thought. I've really nailed this whole magic thing. Do I call LA, or do they call me?

A couple of moments passed. Still nothing.

I couldn't understand. Why weren't they reacting? I had just predicted the future, and was getting nothing back for it. This was the very same audience that had almost exploded with excitement when I made a necklace appear in a balloon.

It was at this point that I thought it might be a smart idea to glance at the scroll. And I have never in my life been more embarrassed.

Because the word written on it was not 'excellent'. It was 'elephant'.

'Erm,' I spluttered.

So close, yet so far. The silence continued. And if there was ever a time when I wanted to curl up in a ball and hibernate, this was it. I had messed up completely. Fifteen minutes of build-up, all for this.

I'd love to tell you that I somehow turned it around, that this was a mistake on purpose – that the actual reveal was still to come and I was about to make a real elephant appear. But no. No such luck. I had no back-up plan, no way out and nowhere to hide.

I can't fully recall what happened next. I was too shaken by the mistake. All I know is that somehow, I wrapped things up, made a joke, got off that stage as quickly as possible and bought myself two McDonald's chocolate milkshakes on the drive home to drown my sorrows.

But there is a silver lining. I was so scarred by the experience that I vowed to always *triple* check everything before setting foot on a stage. And since that frightful night, I've had the joy of successfully pulling off the newspaper prediction many times – so much so that it has regained its former status as my favourite trick. It was even the demonstration that, I'm convinced, landed me a show on BBC. I truly believe that there are no failures – only lessons. It's a cliché, but it's true.

Having said that, I have no desire to repeat that experience. So if you ever see me after a show, and look closely at my wrist, you'll see for yourself, a tiny word written in Sharpie, just below my tattoo. And it'll be the prediction for that night's finale.

Because I'm never getting *that* trick wrong again. I'll just mess something else up instead.

TRICK
TOK
FIVE:
ADOPTING THE
RIGHT MINDSET

Making sure your head is in the right place (and your body, too) is all-important when you're doing stuff online. There is so much hanging on how you project yourself and how you treat – and view – your followers.

STATE

I'm not referring to where you live. No, I'm talking about your own physical and mental state.

When I made the small change I'm going to tell you about, my video quality doubled instantly. It's going to sound hokey and weird, but if you haven't tried this before, you're in for a real treat.

Ever watched one of your favourite creators/actors/musicians and wondered where their infectious energy comes from? Well, in a lot of cases, it's down to them deliberately changing their physical and mental state before a performance. But what does that mean? I'll give you a personal example.

Before I begin filming a video, I make sure that I intentionally open up my posture, warm up my voice and get excited. You see, being good on camera takes a lot of energy, and you can't expect to go from 0–100MPH in one second. So whether it's a case of moving around, acting a bit crazy or even spending a few seconds literally shaking my body around first, I'll do it.

And I'm not the only one. Most of the successful creators I know do the same thing, sometimes consciously, sometimes by instinct. If I ever forget to hype myself up and get into a positive mental and physical state

before filming, you can always tell when watching the footage back.

You can take a 6/10 video to an 8/10 video simply with a little bit of state prep. Likewise, you could take a 10/10 video down to an 8/10 just because your energy isn't right. So make sure you're showing up on camera, prepared and ready to give it your all. Which doesn't mean you should act like a lunatic, but you should be your most expressive and charismatic self. And it's a lot easier to access that part of yourself if you've taken some time to prime your state.

If you want a specific exercise to get you started, try this:
- Just before filming, take a few moments and clap your hands together, as hard as you can, three times.
- Shake it out for a few moments, and you're set.

For me, it helps to have music playing just before I hit 'record', as I find it more motivating.

Experiment, see what gets you excited, then do it. Anything to get the blood flowing and energy going.

Change your state.

FRIENDS, NOT FANS

A lot of people disagree with me on this one.

But I always try to treat my followers as friends. I try my best to reply to every message, even if that ultimately proves impossible.

Treat people the way you would have them treat you. So if someone has taken the time out of their day to send you a nice message, you owe it to them to at least read it. I get that eventually, if you become big enough, sure, you might not get time to see that every single person gets a reply. But if you're reading this, and you don't have hundreds and hundreds of messages flying at you left, right and centre, then try and send the love back.

It only takes one message for you to become someone's favourite creator for life!

FRIENDS OVER FOLLOWERS

As someone who would never have dreamed that I'd one day have over 10 million followers online, I can honestly and wholeheartedly tell you that it's not what you think it'll be like.

Of course, there are all sorts of incredible moments that come from online success. But never make the mistake of assuming that all your followers are real fans. Most of them aren't.

Focus on building true friends and fans, not just followers.

Sure, follower building is a key component to finding those fans in the first place, but trust me, it'd be better to have 100 people who genuinely love and support everything you do, than 10 million who barely know who you are.

QUALITY AND QUANTITY

So what should you shoot for? Quantity or quality? This point is constantly up for debate, but I'll give you my two cents on the topic.

I think that you can – and should – aim for both. However, the thing that people often miss is that it will likely take a lot of quantity for you to figure out how to create quality.

Let's imagine you've never played tennis before. Do you expect to set foot on the court and instantly hit a perfect serve? Most likely not. So why would you expect to be 'perfect' (perfect is impossible by the way, so don't shoot for it – just always be improving) when you create social media content?

It's going to take practice, but over time, with reps, you can become good at making content. The best way to get good is to work hard, but work smart. Put out a lot of content and make use of all the tips and tricks I've taught you here, as well as any others you may come across. Success leaves clues, so make sure to pay attention to what is trending and lean into that.

The truth is, it's probably going to take more work than you expect. So be ready for that. Most people give up before they gather momentum and get good. But armed with this knowledge, you can ensure you don't let that happen to you.

I can't give you a specific number of posts or a time frame to follow, as every situation is different. But keep going; you'll know when you're at the edge of your comfort zone – and that's where the magic happens!

So be constantly striving to improve, but don't kid yourself into thinking that you're only putting out tiny amounts of content because you want it to be *perfect*. Perfectionism is an excuse for you to stay where you are – and you'll never get better unless you accept that you're going to have some bad videos.

Pay attention to what's working and do more of it. Then, once you've put out enough content, quality will come naturally to you. It's a game of gradual improvement and consistency.

But remember, every piece of content that you put out could be the first time that someone discovers you. So although I encourage quantity, always make sure you're trying your best and don't put out content simply for the sake of it.

'KAIZEN' – CHANGE FOR THE BETTER

When people ask me about how to grow on social media, and I give them the advice I've given you, I'm often met with the same response – 'But I don't know how to do any of that stuff'.

They could be talking about any number of things, from editing, to filming, to posting, to idea generation . . . the list goes on and on. And they may well be right – that they don't know how to do *any of that stuff*. But then again, they also didn't know how to ride a bike once. Or swim. Or drive a car. Or cook dinner. But they figured it out.

Don't use your current lack of skills to determine your future results. You can always skill up. And it's not about waking up as an expert tomorrow morning. Rather, it's about intentionally improving a little bit every single day. Gradual, but ongoing improvement.

The key, as I said earlier, is to be persistent. Don't let anything stand in the way of you getting to where you want to be. It's unlikely that you currently possess all the skills you're going to need on your journey, but that doesn't mean you can't work on them. And when you inevitably run into a problem you hadn't anticipated and don't know how to solve it, refocus on where you want to go, not where you currently are.

Behind every success, there are countless failures. I can tell you this from personal experience. And the only reason I've managed to get to where I'm at right now is that when I reached low points, I kept going: where other magicians woke up and decided that they were too tired to film, I went ahead and did it anyway.

I'm certainly not the only person who does this in my industry; in fact, there are others who are even more relentless than me. And their results show it!

So instead of folding like a cheap chair when things don't go your way, focus on improving your skills. As the American entrepreneur Jim Rohn said, 'Don't wish things were easier; wish you were better!'

THE SECRET

I recently read a book all about P. T. Barnum – 'the greatest showman'. While a lot of his actions over the years may be questionable, there's no disputing that he was a master of getting and keeping attention. I imagine if he were alive today, he'd be a social media master.

One thing I learned from Barnum and his spectacular events is that there's a glaringly obvious secret to success when it comes to publicity in any form.

Contrast is the secret.

You have to stand out. If you want proof of this, have a look at the most famous people on the planet. The majority of them have something extremely contrasting or unique about them. Take Robert Downey Jr's dry sense of humour, Trump's hair, a rapper's jewel . . .

I've tried to lean into all the things that make me unique (my crazy hair, my strange clothing choices, high energy, charisma . . .) as much as possible and accentuate them. And you can do the same. Whether that means dressing in a certain way, talking in a particular manner or any number of other possibilities, you need to stand out.

When asked 'What makes a viral video?' one of TikTok's biggest stars put it really nicely, saying, 'Viral is something you wouldn't normally see'.

So simple, yet so true. Contrast is the secret. So do whatever you can to make people say, 'I've never seen something quite like this before!'

CTA

This is something that I did wrong for a long time. Or rather, I didn't do it at all.

So what is a CTA? Simply, 'Call To Action'.

But what does that mean? Well, in this case, it means asking the viewer to take some sort of action, whether that be 'liking' a post, 'following' or 'sharing'.

Here's the thing, it's getting more and more competitive online, and in most cases, unless you're so good that people can't ignore you, most won't take much action at the end of your content. So you need to encourage them. And this could be as straightforward as a brief text box popping up at the end of your video asking for a follow, a share or whatever you like.

This is such a simple fix but one that will make the world of difference. Trust me, the second you start doing it, you'll wish you had started sooner.

It took me two years to grow from zero to a million followers on TikTok without using calls to action. Then it took one month to grow from 1 million to 2 million – because I did use them. You see the power there?

The key is that you do it in a way that isn't too pushy, but also isn't soft. You need to ask directly for what you want. And if your content is really good, then people will be glad you used a CTA. After all, if what you do is great, why wouldn't they want to see more? So be sure to remind people to take action. All the big stars do it; you should, too!

I try to add a call to action in a way that fits in with my content. For example, instead of just blatantly screaming 'FOLLOW ME OR ELSE', I like to add an incentive or a reason: 'Follow for More Magic' or, 'If this trick fools you, hit the follow button . . . deal'. That sort of thing.

Trust me, the last thing you want to happen is for a piece of content to blow up, and you haven't placed a call to action. You're throwing potential fans down the drain. I know, I know, it's more work, and some people might even see it as needy. But it's also the most effective change I've made in order to grow my brand.

So use CTAs.

And with that said, my call to action to you right now, is to keep reading!

THE #1 COMPONENT

Ok, so we've talked about loads and loads of secrets, tactics and the mindset behind succeeding online. But there's one key point that I haven't made. And I wish I had been told this when I started out. You'll find it very, very hard to find this advice online anywhere – not because it's particularly advanced, but because it's glaringly obvious. And it's also by far the most overlooked thing when it comes to social media growth.

The idea is everything.

Read that again.

You see, you could have the best lighting in the world, the best hook, the best call to action, the best everything – but if the core concept of the video isn't a winner by nature, then it doesn't make any difference.

To put it simply: your stuff has to be good.

No – your stuff has to be excellent. I've had the pleasure of helping a bunch of smaller creators grow their accounts, and this is the one thing that they always struggle to grasp. You need to be constantly thinking and developing content ideas that are fantastic. I have three or four sessions a week dedicated to just jotting down ideas on an A4 legal pad. Most of these are truly tragic. Some are ok. And some are great. Those are the ones that I try to give all my attention to.

Please don't waste your time on ideas that nobody will ever find interesting, no matter how hard you work on them. As the old saying goes, 'You can't polish a turd'. Instead, spend time thinking about what *you'd* love to see, and what you think will grab the attention of others.

But why do so few people do this? Because it's hard. It's gruelling, it's challenging and it requires a lot of patience, sifting through all your terrible ideas. But it's worth it. So stop spending so much time on trivialities and focus on the meat and potatoes of your content: the idea itself.

Sure, time of posting is important, hashtags can be helpful, descriptions might give you a little boost . . . but if your content is inherently boring or bad, none of these makes any difference. You need to refocus on the main thing.

AND THERE WE HAVE IT

You now know me just about as well as many of my closest friends. I truly appreciate you taking the time out to read this book – it means more to me than you could possibly know. If you'd told me three years ago that I would write a book and have it published, I would have laughed in your face. But such is life, and I'm eternally grateful to you for helping me along in my journey. It's been a real joy to write the book, and I hope you've enjoyed it. I also hope that you have – at the very least – learned a few tricks and had a good laugh at my expense!

As you now know, I may not be the perfect magician, but having persevered through all those awkward encounters, failures and mishaps, picking myself up every time I fell down, I can tell you one thing: if you want to do something, go for it. The failures are worth it. So if you have a talent, an obsession or any calling at all, you owe it not only to yourself but to the rest of the world to give it your best shot.

I'm no more talented, smart or lucky than you. If this opportunity has been available to me, it's available to you, too. And remember, above everything else: have fun while you're doing all this. After all, if you aren't enjoying the process, then what's the point?

I've given you the best tools I know of to grow a social media account. With the fast-paced nature of the internet, things are always changing. However, the general mindset that I've laid out for you should stand you in good stead, despite the changes taking place on any given platform.

I've been told my entire life that becoming a magician is risky, impractical, a mere pipe dream. At only twenty-three, I know for a fact that my understanding of how the world works is extremely limited, but this I do know: had I listened to those people, I would have missed out on all the amazing memories and experiences that make me me.

I believe in you. So, get started! Go after what you love, work hard and never give up. Ever.

Now, let's finish this thing the way we started – with a puzzle.

What do you call a magic owl?

Whodini.

On second thoughts – I think I'll stick to magic.

GLOSSARY

Complete cut A basic cutting of the deck, taking the upper half of the cards off the top, then placing the bottom stack on top.

CTA (Call to action) A piece of content intended to induce a viewer, reader or listener to perform a specific act.

False overhand shuffle A means of maintaining control over the top or bottom card of the deck.

Forcing a card A method of controlling a choice made by a spectator during a trick.

Hook Something designed to catch people's attention.

Human blockhead An illusion in which the performer hammers a nail (or other dangerous object) into their nostril.

Hypnosis Inducing a state of consciousness in which a person apparently loses the power of voluntary action and is highly responsive to suggestion or direction.

Instant handshake induction A hypnotic pattern interrupt used to induce someone into a trance state.

Key card principle Making use of one playing card so as to keep track of another.

Levitation The action of rising or causing something to rise and hover in the air, typically by means of supposed magical powers.

Mentalism The theory that physical and psychological phenomena are ultimately explicable only in terms of a creative and interpretative mind.

Misdirection The action or process of directing someone to the wrong place or in the wrong direction.

Palming This refers to the concealment of an object in your hand, so that it is entirely covered.

Platform A social media platform is an application or website through which users are able to create, access and share content and find and connect with other users.

Prestidigitator Another name for the speedy hand movements and mysterious techniques of an illusionist.

Reveal Making previously unknown or secret information known to others.

Rising card A playing card seemingly singles itself out from among all the other cards.

Sleight of hand Manual dexterity, typically in performing conjuring tricks.

Suggestibility The quality of being inclined to accept and act on the suggestions of others.

Telekenesis The supposed ability to move objects at a distance by mental power or other non-physical means.

Teleporting To transport or be transported across space and distance instantly.

Traffic In internet terms, this refers to web users who visit a website.

Watch time The total amount of time in aggregate that viewers spend watching your videos.

ACKNOWLEDGEMENTS

This book would not have been possible without the help of the amazing people around me. The amount of love and support shown to me over the years has been astronomical, and I'll always be grateful for that.

For my own selfish peace of mind ... these are in no particular order.

To Lucy. This book wouldn't exist without you. I probably would have given up years ago without your constant kindness and support. Thank you for being there for me through everything. Love you.

Ethan. Thank you, not for being my brother (because let's face it ... you didn't have a choice in the matter) but for being my closest friend, my biggest supporter and one of the only people I can be entirely myself around.

Shane Gillen. You saw something in me that nobody else did, including myself. Thank you for always pushing me, believing in me and being the kindest person I know. I look up to you enormously.

Mum, for the years and years of nurturing my talents, and for teaching me that the more you put in, the more you get out. Our coffee dates are the best.

Emma, thanks for always being the one to celebrate my wins and make me feel seen. Your actions speak louder than everyone else's words.

Dad. I have always been proud to be your son, but I become more and more so the older I get. Thank you for teaching me that being kind is the greatest magic there is. (I hope you actually read this book, unlike the thousands of others you have stacked up in the attic!)

The chums. Nobody makes me laugh like you guys do. You're family.

Sharon and Mark. You've done more for me than you could possibly imagine ... and are kind to a fault. You're my family.

Beau Cremer and Tom Elderfield. I'm jealous of both of your magical brains. You guys are the definition of selfless and I brag about being friends with you.

Dan Rhodes. They say you shouldn't keep yes men around, but I prefer to keep one. Dan, you make me feel like I can do anything, even on the hardest days.

Nana and Papa, thank you for making me feel special, and for always showing up to my shows. For buying my first magic tricks and never making me feel like magic was a waste of time.

Christopher Jordan. You have always been like a big brother to me... thanks for being the first person to film videos with me. Let's hope nobody ever finds them!

Tom Smyth, thank you for your relentless energy. I've never met someone with as much passion as you, and it inspired me to sit down and get this book written with massive positive energy.

Kymann Power. Thank you for always showing up for me, since the beginning. You've been so selfless in helping me share my magic with the world, I love dreaming big with you.

Greg, thank you for making me feel like anything is possible and for giving me a chance when nobody else did.

HarperCollins. Thank you for believing in my magical message and for giving me this incredible opportunity. I've never been more excited to work on a project, and you've made it effortless. Holly and Kelly, you made me feel like what I was writing mattered. Thank you to Georgina, James, Louise, Hattie and Lucy too!

Nanny and Granda. I wish Granda was here to read this... but I like to imagine he'd be proud! Thank you for sitting through hours and hours (and hours) of terrible magic tricks, and never making me feel like an annoyance. Nanny, the years growing up at your house shaped me into my unusual, creative self. When I think of my childhood, I think of you.

Chas, thank you for your feedback on this book along the way. As a first-time author your confidence in me made a massive difference.

Isabella, Meg, Murphy, Lola, Doris and Norman. You're a reminder that there is endless good in the world. You make everything better.